AF511846

The Philosophical Understanding of Human Rights

The Philosophical Understanding of Human Rights

Benulal Dhar

PRINTWORLD
Publishers of Indian Traditions

Cataloging in Publication Data — DK
[Courtesy: D.K. Agencies (P) Ltd. <docinfo@dkagencies.com>]

Dhar, Benulal.
The philosophical understanding of human rights / Benulal Dhar.
p. cm.
Reprint.
Includes bibliographical references (p.) and index.
ISBN 13: 9788124607145

1. Human rights – Philosophy. I. Title.

DDC 323.01 23

© **Benulal Dhar**
ISBN 13: 978-81-246-0714-5
First published in India in 2013

All rights reserved. No part of this publication may be reproduced or transmitted, except brief quotations, in any form or by any means, electronic or mechanical, including photocopying, recording, or any information storage or retrieval system, without prior written permission of the copyright holder, indicated above, and the publishers.

Printed and published by:
D.K. Printworld (P) Ltd.
Regd. office : *"Vedaśrī,"* F-395, Sudarshan Park
(Metro Station: Ramesh Nagar)
New Delhi - 110 015
Phones : (011) 2545 3975, 2546 6019; *Fax* : (011) 2546 5926
e-mail : indology@dkprintworld.com
Web : www.dkprintworld.com

To

the memory
of my father

Late Naresh Chandra Dhar

who always wanted me
to be a learned man

Preface

It is now generally agreed that the present social, political and economic orders all over the globe are needed to be based on some conception of the rights of man, and this is to ensure the minimum security and justice to the life of people suffered by violence and oppression. Human rights provide a shield to safeguard human individual or group of individuals from all sorts of arbitrariness and tyranny caused by the state or other agents and aim at transforming the present world into a better and a more just world. Keeping in view this practical urgency, the more stress is laid on the application of human rights, i.e. is, how the violations of various human rights can be prevented or how the rights can be implemented in people's lives than on critically understanding the concept itself and problems it involves at theoretical or philosophical level. Under the immense pressure of rescuing people from injustice and tyranny, the philosophical problems are often ignored or kept in abeyance. In order to remedy the situation, a modest attempt has been made in the present study to identify and analyse the central issues contained in the rich philosophical tradition of human rights beginning with early modern period to contemporary times.

Having given an account of the origins and historical development of the idea of human rights, the present study analyses the doctrine of natural rights and its critiques, and assesses the world-view that has affected its formulations. The work also presents a clear exposition of some contemporary theories of rights developed independently of the natural rights paradigm as also the theories wherein the conception of rights is found to be compatible with utilitarianism. And while briefly arguing for discursive understanding of human rights based on the diversity of morals that is embedded in different cultural traditions of the world and for reconstruction of the conception of human rights in more inclusive and cross-cultural terms, the present work analyses the conception of human dignity from the Vedāntic perspective as a case study, which is regarded as an important underlying principle of human rights.

A preface is perhaps the only place in a study where one can strike a personal note. My own interest in the philosophy of human rights dates from 1997, the year in which I came in touch with Association for Protection of Democratic Rights (APDR) based in the state of West Bengal, India. This organization works for democratic and human rights generally independently but sometimes in coagulation with other non-state groups and bodies. As a well-wisher member of this human and democratic rights body, I have always been more focused on the philosophical dimension of human rights than involved in its activism. Accordingly, I have been engaged in collecting study materials from different libraries as also in reading and writing on the topic, which have been going on at a very slow pace. The present work is the outcome of my intellectual exercise with the idea of human rights during all these years.

Benulal Dhar

Contents

Acknowledgement

At the outset, I would naturally give grateful thanks to my teacher Prof. Ranjan K. Ghosh, formerly Director (P&R), Indian Council of Philosophical Research, New Delhi and Head, Department of Philosophy, North Bengal University, who has always been a source of encouragement and support for over two decades. I owe a debt of gratitude to Prof. Rakesh Chandra, Department of Philosophy, Lucknow University, for his kind help in making me the subject understood well. Prof. Kantilal Das and Prof. Jyotish Chandra Basak, Department of Philosophy, North Bengal University, always appreciate my intellectual endeavours. I avail this opportunity to thank them. I gratefully acknowledge the help received from Prof. Morton E. Winston, Chair, Department of Philosophy and Director, Alan Dawley Center for the Study of Social Justice, The College of New Jersey, USA, who was kind enough to send me a copy of his book as also his published articles addressed to the philosophy of human rights. I received many helpful ideas and insights relating to the present topic from my friend Dr Aziz Ahmed, Department of Political Science, Falakata College, Jalpaiguri. I thank Dr N.S. Das, Principal, Sukanta Mahavidyalaya and all my colleagues there, who have always been supportive and helpful in my various academic endeavours. I also avail this opportunity to thank all the members of APDR for participating on different occasions in informal debates involving various theoretical issues on human rights, helping me to keep myself intellectually alive.

I wish to place on record my debt of gratitude to the University Grants Commission (UGC) for a grant under the scheme "Minor Research Project" for carrying out this research work. I also thank the authorities of Sukanta Mahavidyalaya for granting me a study leave for eight weeks, which made my task easier and pleasanter. For using the library facilities during this period of research, I owe several debts of gratitude, especially to: (i) North Bengal University Library; (ii) Indian Council of Philosophical Research Library, Lucknow; (iii) Ramkrishna Mission Institute of Culture, Kolkata; (iv) Indian Institute of Advanced Study, Shimla; (v) American Center Library, Kolkata; (vi) National Library, Kolkata; (vii) North-Eastern Hill University Library; and (viii) Lucknow University Library.

Thanks are also due to the editorial team of D.K. Printworld for making considerable improvement upon the original script and to Shri Susheel K. Mittal for the execution of its publication.

And, finally, I give my heartfelt thanks to my wife, Rekha, who has often waived off her right to personal comfort, paving the way for my intellectual endeavours. The lively and cheerful mood of my two dear children, Rajarshi and Shreosee, has always been an eloquent and unfailing source of encouragement.

Benulal Dhar

1

Introduction

HUMAN rights are now one of the animated subjects of study and discussion from various perspectives, such as legal, political, historical and, of course, philosophical in view of their widespread application in the social, political and economic life of people in recent times all over the globe. As an operative idea of today's life, the discourse of human rights is mainly oriented towards activism. The horror of Second World War has given the impetus to be more concerned with the practice of human rights in the social, political and economic life of people. And in order to reinforce this effort, UN Declaration of Human Rights, 1948 was adopted. This document is a systematic attempt to secure universal recognition of a wide range of human rights all over the world. Thus all these efforts were focused upon activism rather than on raising philosophical issues relating to the nature, content and justification of human rights. But the concept of human rights has a rich philosophical or theoretical tradition which cannot be ignored. The philosophical dimension of the idea of human rights deserves proper attention. For, in the latter lies the scientific basis of its practice. Though the Western moral and political philosophers from ancient times down to the present era have put forward many theories, and raised many questions and problems with regard to human rights, its philosophical domain is not yet exhausted. Philosophical issues like old habits die hard. On the one hand, the age-old challenges relating to human rights continue to haunt the present-day philosophers, they are also raising path-breaking questions in view of the emergence of innovative ideas and alterations in the context and temper of modern society and politics on the other. It is in this context of broadening outlook that it is worthwhile to look back on the broad conspectus of human rights theories and ideas. Besides, the claim for human rights to be accepted as *universal* norm by one and all societies and cultures of the world has also set the stage for critically analysing the relevance of this operative notion as a Western cultural construct to *other* cultures. Therefore the challenges and issues that are raised by philosophers with regard to human rights in the changing context of society, morality, culture and politics call for a thorough philosophical analysis and critical examination in order to grapple afresh with the whole gamut of practical issues relating to them. The present work proposes to move in this direction.

The Challenges

Some of the challenges to be addressed with in the present study would include:

1. What are rights in general, and what are human rights in particular?
2. What are the distinctive features of human rights that distinguish them from other rights?
3. How the notion of natural rights is distinguished from contemporary concept of human rights?
4. What features of human beings justify the claim that they are entitled to have some intrinsic and inalienable rights?
5. Can human rights represent a universal moral standard?

6. Are cultures, other than the Western, potential grounds for developing some such conceptions of rights on their own?

Above all, this work presents the diverse perspectives and philosophical controversies on rights, which will help readers to understand what constitute human rights and how they occupy an essential place in our contemporary social and political life.

What Does Philosophical Understanding Mean?

Let us now proceed by asking a crucial question: What does it mean by the philosophical understanding of human rights?

First, the primary task of any philosophical approach to human rights, for that matter, to any topic, is to lay bare the meaning of the concept itself, which at its first encounter with us is likely to remain obscure and unintelligible. Philosophic endeavour makes explicit what is implicit, and exposes what is covered up. So the understanding of human rights from the philosophical perspective means to become clearly aware of the vague and unconscious assumptions underlying the idea, which are operative in our lives and guide our practical actions relating to it. It is essential that we discover these assumptions lying behind the conception if we do not want to be driven *blindly* in our effort to implement the idea in the social and political life. In short, it is the expository effort of philosophy that would clarify the presuppositions of human rights conception, and thereby it would deepen our understanding of its truth.

Second, many of us are not free from prejudices and misconceptions about the concept of human rights, especially because it is rooted in a foreign culture, i.e. in the Western culture. It is needed that the philosophical theories of human rights are to be submitted to critical examination by rational means in order to dispel all prejudices and misconceptions about the notion, and ensure that its application would not be pernicious to our social and political life. The philosophical treatment of human rights would make it clear that this idea is not a myth that has come down to us as part of social customs and mores but has a strong rational foundation of its own. While making critical analysis, this approach takes into consideration the arguments both for and against the conception.

Third, the philosophical study of human rights takes a comprehensive view of the world rather than a parochial one while in search of the truth of a conception. It makes an attempt to understand the idea in its multiple dimensions. In other words, what it means to have the rights of man from the social, political, moral and other perspectives? is the question that engages a philosopher. The philosophical approach enlightens our common-sense idea about it as well as broadens the overall human perspective on the subject. It also makes people realize how emotionally attached they are to the belief in the idea of human rights when it comes under the philosophical scrutiny.

Fourth, in order to adopt human rights as a public policy in the social and political life it is imperative that it passes the test of philosophical scrutiny. As Martha Nussbaum has rightly pointed out,

> . . . philosophers are badly needed in academic deliberations about public policy, as critical scrutinizers of arguments and as obsessive pursuers of the foundational concepts and questions. For here, if anywhere, it is important to seek rigour and conceptual clarity.[1]

Last, another important function of philosophy is to provide justification for any belief. And in this case that human beings

[1] M.C. Nussbaum, "Public Philosophy and International Feminism" in C.P. Ragland and Sarah Heidt (eds.) *What Is Philosophy?*, New Haven: Yale University Press, 2001, pp. 132-33.

should be treated in certain ways involves various perspectives in understanding the human individual and his relationships with his fellow-beings, and it is only the philosophical approach that can address the various issues relating to the nature of human beings, and provides justifications for the possession of inherent and inalienable rights.

A Definition and Initial Characterizations of Human Rights

The concept of rights, like such other notions as equality, liberty and justice, has its origin in the liberal tradition of the West. The liberal thinkers explain the concept of rights on the basis of their understanding of human nature. It is their conception of human nature that determines the commitment to moral and political values including rights. In the liberal tradition, human beings are regarded as individuals who are prior to any social organization, and they, as individuals, take moral priority over any collective good. So rights belong to human beings as individuals, although there are some exceptional liberal thinkers (such as T.H. Green) according to whom rights belong to man only in community with others.

We may now make some initial characterizations of human rights, though in detailed treatment of them we would see that there is no consensus among the philosophers as to their nature. Indeed, the main task of the present study is to discuss the diverse ways in which rights are understood by philosophers. Generally speaking, human rights secure and protect some important interests of an individual against the state or other agents, and thereby give him something to stand on. To possess human rights means that one is entitled to be treated in a way that is beneficial to him. Rights provide an individual a shield to protect himself from all forms of morally unjustified invasion by the state or other agents. An individual is in urgent need of private space to protect his essential human attributes and thereby facilitating him to grow and develop in physical, psychological, moral, aesthetic and spiritual terms. And this security and protection is supposed to be provided by the rights. Accordingly, we may define human rights as follows:

> A human right is a conceptual mechanism that is meant for securing and protecting a private space for an individual or a group of individuals to nurture his or their certain essential human attributes, such as physical, psychical, intellectual, moral, aesthetic, and spiritual, leading to the realization of all human potentialities, and it calls for determinate actions towards maintaining the fenced off domain for individual or group of individuals.

The point is that rights are invoked in order to provide an individual a private space for adequate functioning as a human being. Rights provide him a fenced off domain to protect his essential human attributes and thereby pave the way for him to realize all his potentialities as a human being.

Human rights are understood as a kind of *moral* rights, which belong to all individuals simply by virtue of being human, irrespective of any distinction, such as race, sex, language, religion, nationality or other status. This proposition states some essential conditions of what is meant by human rights. First, human rights are the subset of *moral* rights as distinguished from *legal* rights. These rights are nowadays supported by UN Declaration of Human Rights, 1948. Many countries have given some of the rights that have found place in the *Declarations* or *Bills of Rights* the legal status in their constitutions. Thus human rights are given recognition and protection by the laws of particular states, and this being so, an individual becomes able to influence and control the actions of his fellow-citizens, even the unjustified actions of the state. The laws of the state stand behind and entitle him to make such a claim upon other citizens or even upon the state itself. However, the persons, who belong to the countries that have not given these rights the legal status, are not thereby deprived of such rights. It is essential part of the contemporary notion of human rights that the latter belong to all persons irrespective of their nationalities which might not have recognized and guaranteed them.

The moral force of human rights is in no way curbed by the non-recognition of them by any state, and they belong universally, inherently, or inalienably to all persons. Indeed, all moral rights are not always recognized or guaranteed by the laws of a state. The persons lacking legal assistance to protect their human rights can justifiably continue to claim these rights as *moral* rights. It is the moral force of such rights that is inherent in the idea of human rights, and it is the moral ground that provides a person to stand on to claim rights. Thus, to claim a human right is not to ask for a favour or to express a mere wish, but to place a moral claim to something and against someone. The rights not to be tortured or not to be arbitrarily confined are claims that have inherent *moral* force, though they may not have *legal* force. And the addressee of these human rights may be a government, a person, or a group of persons. If these claims are not responded to appropriately by the government or other agencies, then this constitutes a grave affront to justice.

Second, human rights are birthrights and not acquired by performing some deeds or for having placed in certain situation. For example, the right of a publisher who acquires it through signing a contract with an author, or the right of a teacher who enjoys his right for having placed in a special position of teaching. Human rights, like these rights, are neither acquired nor limited to some persons. They are *not* linked to person's duties or positions but are universally owed to him because of the very fact that he is a human person. These rights inalienably and intrinsically pertain to each and every person. That is, they cannot be voluntarily renounced or transferred. To deprive an individual of these rights in exchange of other goods would mean *dehumanization* of the individual. Rights are invoked in order to protect the inherent dignity of the human person.

However, there is no consensus among philosophers regarding the nature, content and justification of human rights. The view of a philosopher may coincide with that of another partially but not wholly. The main reason for disagreements among philosophers is that philosophical truths about human rights, or for that matter, about any topic are neither natural nor scientific facts the nature of which could be decided on the basis of observation or experiment. The nature of philosophical problems, including those relating to human rights, is such that they can only be clarified to a certain extent, but cannot be solved once and for all by means of philosophical reflections.

Now, the question is: What are these rights the philosophy of which we shall be analysing in the present study? It is customary to consider human rights as having evolved in the three generations:

1. The *first* generation rights are referred to as civil and political rights, and have their origins in the Enlightenment and liberal thought in the eighteenth century. These rights are generally couched in the language of natural rights, in the sense that these rights are taken to be enjoyed by individuals as natural endowment. These rights include the right to freedom of expression, the right to free assembly, the right to equality before the law, the right to privacy, the right to vote, the right to practise any religion of choice, the right to be treated with dignity, the right to be treated

without discrimination, and so on. These rights call for protection and guarantee rather than their realization. The state is required to ensure that these rights are not threatened or violated. These rights are referred to as the negative rights. For, these rights impose negative obligations on the state to refrain from interfering with the exercise of these rights.

2. The *second* generation of human rights is known as economic, social and cultural rights. These rights belong to the individual or group to receive various social benefits or services for his/their growth and development. Examples of these rights are: the right to adequate food and clothing, the right to education, the right to employment, the right to health care, the right to social security, and many other rights. Unlike the first generation rights, these rights call for the duty of the state to ensure their *realization* rather than their protection and guarantee.
3. The *third* generation rights are collective in nature, i.e. they belong to a community, group, or nation rather than to an individual, although the individuals are the beneficiary of their realization. These rights include the right to development, the right to environment, the right to self-determination, etc.

The Subject Matter and Plan of the Work

Let us now turn to introduce in brief the subject matter and plan of the work in a systematic and orderly manner that is to be followed in the book. The term "human rights" has its ancestral home in what is known as the natural rights tradition of the West, and descended from the idea of natural rights. Though some philosophers use the term interchangeably but some arguably distinguish the one from the other. It seems to be quite reasonable that the term "natural" is not only replaced by "human" as an adjective of "rights" but also have undergone a change in what is originally meant by it in the history of ideas. While they share some common characteristics, they are also conceptually distinguishable from each other. The present work begins with a brief account of the origins and historical development of the idea of what is known today as human rights.

The concept of natural rights takes two different courses of development in the history of political philosophy. The direction of its first development with a modern perspective is given by Thomas Hobbes. And the second way, in which the natural rights are conceived, is represented by John Locke. The latter conception inspired the American and French Declarations of Rights, and it was also from this conception of natural rights that today's idea of human rights has evolved. And inspired by the ideology of the French Revolution, Thomas Paine espouses the fundamental premises of the Lockean theory of natural rights in formulating his own conception of rights. Though both Hobbes and Locke inaugurate the two distinct traditions of the conception of rights, they along with Paine are guided by the same world-view to work out their respective theories of natural rights. But the popularity of the doctrine of natural rights began to decline when the thinkers like Edmund Burke, Jeremy Bentham and Karl Marx developed their critiques against the doctrine. In this study, we would provide a clear exposition of these natural rights theories and their critiques along with an assessment of the world-view that has shaped the formulation of the theories of natural rights.

The present study makes an attempt to analyse some contemporary theories of rights developed independently of the natural rights paradigm, which are presented by T.H. Green, Margaret MacDonald, Carl Wellman, Joel Feinberg and Rex Martin. Green defines rights as recognized claims;

MacDonald analyses rights as taking a stand; Wellman develops the idea of rights as constellation of Hohfeldian elements; Feinberg argues for rights as claims *to* something and *against* someone; and Martin conceives rights as recognized entitlements. This work also delineates the two present-day theories developed by D.G. Ritchie and David Lyons, wherein rights are found to be compatible with utilitarianism. And, finally, while arguing for discursive understanding of human rights based on the diversity of morals that is embedded in the different cultural traditions of the world, the present study explicates the idea of human dignity from the Kantian and the Vedāntic perspectives.

Having explained what does the philosophical understanding mean and introduced the problems and subject matter of this study in this chapter, we would now proceed to concern ourselves in Chapter 2 with the origins and historical development of the idea of human rights. Chapter 3 makes an attempt to give a clear exposition of the natural rights theories expounded by three modern thinkers, namely, Hobbes, Locke and Paine. Chapter 4 deals with the critiques of natural rights developed by Bentham, Burke, Marx, Ritchie and MacDonald. Chapter 5 makes an assessment of the world-view which has shaped the formulation of natural rights doctrine. Chapter 6 analyses some contemporary theories of rights which are developed independently of the natural rights school. Chapter 7 is devoted to the arguments from utility. And the concluding Chapter 8 argues for discursive approach to human rights and analyses the concept of human dignity as an underlying principle of human rights from the Kantian and the Vedāntic perspectives.

2

The Idea of Human Rights
Its Origins and Historical Development

THE term "human rights" is of recent origin. Earlier, it was known variously as "the natural rights", "the rights of man" and "the civil rights". Though the historical roots of the notion can be traced back to the ancient Greek and medieval philosophies, it has been developed into a full-fledged theoretical form with a modern perspective in the seventeenth- and eighteenth-century European political thought, which is known as the natural rights tradition. As a progeny of the natural-rights school, the conception of rights has exercised a powerful and pervasive influence over the subsequent understanding of rights. Before following this significant development of the idea, let us turn for a while to trace its philosophical lineage to the Greek and medieval teachings.

Rights: Tracing the Philosophical Lineage to the Ancient and Medieval World

It is widespread a notion since the antiquity that there is a law which is different from the law of the state rulers, and more binding and superior than the law of the state. The former is regarded as the "unwritten law of heaven", and the latter is merely a human contrivance. It is the Stoics who first employed the concept of natural law to state that all men stand on equal footing for having possessed of the same natural reason. The idea of natural law finds one of the earliest and most persuasive expressions in Greek poet Sophocles' play *Antigone.* In course of arguments and counter-arguments between Creon, the king of Thebes and Antigone, the sister of deceased Polynices, Sophocles strives to send out a strong message that justice should be allowed to prevail even if it goes against the man-made laws. While transgressing the law of the state and being crushed by it, Antigone claims to have had her rights that are bestowed by the unwritten and eternal law of heaven. This law is identified by the philosophers and thinkers as "natural law". The concept of natural law together with natural rights is said to have been figured in the context of Aristotle's theory of natural justice. Epictectus, a Greek Stoic philosopher, has dealt at some length with the notion of freedom which is one of the core human rights claimed in the modern world. He seems to have made an attempt to define the notion in the following words:

> He is free who lives as he likes, who is not subject to compulsion, to restraint, or to violence; whose pursuits are unhindered, his desires successful, his aversions unincurred.[1]

The Roman statesman and lawyer Cicero has based his idea of law regulating human conduct and of justice on "Nature". He writes:

> Law is the highest reason, implanted in Nature, which commands what ought to be done and forbids the opposite.[2]

He adds,

> But out of all the material of the philosophers' discussions, surely there comes nothing more valuable than the full realization that we are born for Justice, and that right is based, not upon men's opinions, but upon Nature.[3]

---

1 Epictectus, "The Discourses", in Macheline R. Ishay (ed.) *The Human Rights Reader,* London: Routledge, 1997, p. 29.

2 Cicero, "The Laws", in *The Human Rights Reader,* p. 24.

3 Ibid., p. 25.

The idea of nature and natural law has been given even a greater role in human affairs by the medieval Christian scholastics – notably by the Italian theologian and philosopher St. Thomas Aquinas (1224-74). Natural law is understood by him as general moral principle laid down by God, which is the basis of right human conduct. It is discovered by reason. Though the idea of natural law is postulated to be a divine underlying principle of the universe, it constitutes a yardstick for evaluating political regime together with its "positive" laws enacted by humankind. In this divine scheme, each person – the ruler and the subjects alike – is subject to the natural law.

Thus the idea of natural law so far was based entirely on the Christian theism that required belief in a deity as its justificatory ground. It is only at the beginning of the European Enlightenment era after CE 1500 that the notion of natural law became increasingly free of medieval theological trappings. The first move towards restating the notion of natural law in somewhat secular and rational terms is found in the writings of Dutch jurist and political thinker Hugo Grotius (1583–1645). He demonstrates for the first time that it is possible to ascertain all rules by the application of "right reason "without necessarily believing in a Supreme Being. Though God is still the ultimate source of the natural law, Grotius provides a philosophical framework for the treatment of it. For him, the natural law cannot be invalidated even if God is taken to have no existence. Rejecting the expediency as the source of just and fair, he finds the roots of morality in human sociability organized in consonance with his rational nature. Grotius states:

> For the very nature of man, which even if we had no lack of anything would lead us into the mutual relations of society, is the mother of the law of nature.[4]

---

[4] H. Grotius, "On Laws of War and Peace", in *The Human Rights Reader*, p. 75.

The nature of man, being the source of natural law, enables him to join his fellow-men in order to gratify his impelling desire for society. Thus having grounded the existence of natural law in man's social and intelligent nature, he identifies such natural rights as the theft is forbidden, the obligation to fulfil one's promises and inflicting punishment to the criminals. He conceives of *ius*, the Latin word for law, as prescribing the rules of conduct for both individuals and nations. While affirming the sociability of human nature, Grotius recognizes the individuality in the domain of rights. He claims that the sociability of human nature commands respect for individual rights. But what is lacking in Grotian theory, as Richard Tuck points out, is an ethical theory backed by a plausible individualistic psychology.[5] The first philosopher who responded immediately to fill in this historical lacuna was John Selden, a junior contemporary of Grotius. However, a detailed response in this direction was awaited till Thomas Hobbes. But the fact remains that it is the gradual refinement of the Grotian view of natural law and right that is ultimately transmuted into the conception of individual rights in the writings of Enlightenment thinkers.

The Idea of Natural Rights: Historical Development in the Modern Period

The task of developing the idea of rights into a theoretical structure was undertaken by the major figures of European Enlightenment, such as Thomas Hobbes (1588–1679) and John Locke (1632–1704). And this tradition was joined 100 years later by the eighteenth-century political thinker and activist Thomas Paine (1737–1809). The common thread that runs through the Enlightenment thinking on rights is that human beings possess certain inherent or "natural" rights in a

---

[5] R. Tuck, *Natural Rights Theories: Their Origin and Development*, Cambridge: Cambridge University Press, 1979, p. 82.

hypothetical "state of nature" – men's pre-social condition – in the absence of a government. But there were none to safeguard these rights that were crucial for human survival. It is to guarantee the natural rights to the people that there arises the need to the formation of a government by a "social contract", and the legitimacy of the government is derived from its willingness and ability to protect these inherent rights of its subjects. The concept of natural rights is thus given a pivotal role in political affairs in this era.

It is customary to begin the modern analysis of rights with Hobbes, as his theory of rights contains what are considered to be some of the modern features of rights. He presents his theory of rights as part of a political theory in his *Leviathan*, first published in 1651. Among the features that are recognized by Hobbes, the individuality in the area of rights is a part of emerging liberal thought. It is for articulating this and other such modern features of rights that Hobbes deserves to be treated as a precursor of today's analysis of rights. But this usual practice of taking Hobbes as the starting-point of rights-analysis though correct from this perspective, it is regarded as misleading as well. For, Hobbes does not situate the discourse of rights firmly within the emerging liberal tradition as his theory contains some illiberal features, such as for him, rights emanate from all-powerful sovereign state. It is for the latter reason that he is not regarded as part of liberal tradition, which has actually kick-started the modern debates on rights. Hence, his view on rights is regarded by some writers as "premodern".[6]

Hobbes conceives a condition of mankind in what he calls "the state of nature". For him, the life of men in the state of nature was "solitary, poor, nasty, brutish and short". And

---

[6] I. Shapiro, *The Evolution of Rights in Liberal Theory*, Cambridge: Cambridge University Press, 1986, p. 24.

this human predicament in the state of nature, according to him, lies with human nature. Hobbes identifies human nature as appetitive and passionate. In such a natural condition, men possess what he calls "the right of nature" which has only one purpose, i.e. to preserve his own life. The self-preservation is identified by Hobbes as the supreme right, and men reserve the right to take any means for their self-preservation. Further, Hobbes distinguishes this conception of right from law, that is, "the right of nature" from "the law of nature". A right of nature or a natural right consists in liberty to or abstain from doing anything for his own preservation but a law of nature or a natural law states an obligation or precept which forbids doing anything that destroys his life and takes away the means of self-preservation. Like other natural rights thinkers, he does not regard the natural right as derivative of a natural law. Rather, for him, one cannot have both a right and a law to the same thing. That is, one makes the other impossible.

Locke is regarded as the principal exponent of the doctrine of natural law and natural rights, which he has presented in his *Two Treatises of Government*, first published in 1689. He endorses the contemporary view that the natural rights are rights that are enjoyed by men in the state of nature in absence of a government. Unlike Hobbes, he regards the natural rights as derivative of natural law which is a God-given and universal moral principle applicable to the rulers and subjects alike. This natural law is discovered by reason. Locke argues that human beings are endowed by nature with these inherent rights – the right to life, liberty and property – which none can remove or abrogate. As the uncertainties of human life in the state of nature were not favourable in guaranteeing these rights, men entered into a social contract or "compact" to form a political system whose primary task would be to safeguard the rights of people. But Locke, unlike Hobbes, is against granting absolute power to any government, and thereby allowing it to invade individual's sphere of private interests. In fact, he emphasizes that the legitimacy of any government would depend on its willingness and ability to safeguard these rights that men are supposed to have generally enjoyed in the state of nature. The distinctive features of Locke's doctrine of rights include: (i) Human beings are autonomous and capable of exercizing choice by rational means; (ii) they possess inherent rights by virtue of their humanity; and (iii) the legitimacy of any political system solely depends on its willingness and ability to protect these natural rights. These features of Lockean theory of rights have far-reaching influences as the language of subsequent Declarations and Covenants of human rights is couched mostly in Lockean terms.

In his *The Rights of Man* (1791-92) and other writings, Thomas Paine presents his defence of "the rights of man" as reactions to Burke's attack against the French Revolution. His arguments for the rights of man are shaped by the Lockean ideas as well as by the Enlightenment rationalism. Like Locke, Paine believes in the capacity of human reason to resolve social problems, and to discover the law of nature. For him, human beings inherently possess natural rights in the state of nature until the formation of governments. What are distinctive of Paine's ideas on rights include:

1. Unlike Locke, Paine argues against the exercise of state's power over individual's religious beliefs;
2. for Paine, government is to be a contract between sovereign individuals who uniformly decide to subordinate some of their individual rights to social order rather than between rulers and the subjects as Locke proposes; and
3. he makes a distinction between natural rights which are enjoyed by individual on his own and the civil rights which are exchanged in favour of the formation of a social order.

Besides, citing the French "Declaration of the Rights of Man and the Citizen" of 1789, he identifies the rights of man as the rights to liberty, property, security and resistance to oppression as fundamental human rights. All other rights, such as the freedom of speech and the right to choose a government are derivative of the above-mentioned core rights. The significance of Paine's contribution to the understanding of rights does not lie in his philosophical originality, but in his strong defence of the Enlightenment and Lockean ideas relating to rights. As Freeden observes:

> . . . Paine's contribution to the natural-rights tradition was not as an innovator but as a popularizer who made the tradition accessible.[7]

The Idea of Natural Rights: Some Critical Responses

In spite of the profound impact of the theories of natural rights upon subsequent development of the philosophy of rights it began to provoke critical responses from various perspectives by the end of the eighteenth century. Among those who contributed to this process of critical reactions are Edmund Burke (1741–97), Jeremy Bentham (1748–1832) and Karl Marx (1818-83). In the first place, Burke refutes the major premises of the theory of natural rights as embodied in the French "Declaration of the Rights of Man and the Citizen" in his *Reflections on the Revolution in France,* first published in 1790, mainly on three grounds:

1. He argues that the idea of rights of man is an abstract conception and hence meaningless. The rights that are supposed to have been enjoyed by men in the state of nature are not "real" rights but "imagined" ones. For

---

[7] M. Freeden, *Rights,* Delhi: World View Publications, Indian repr., 1998, p. 18.

him, rights cannot evolve out independently of social framework. According to Burke, it is the social interaction that shapes any concept and its practices in life. These apparently revolutionary ideas are not derived from the realization of the complexities of existing societies, and hence they are not the result of shared historical experiences;

2. Burke points out that the rights are social in origin. That is, there cannot be any rights in abstraction from the context of particular society as they have been conceived of by natural rights thinkers. Social and political circumstances determine the distinctive character of rights; and
3. The idea of the rights of man is an untested political proposal. Their application might have practical effect of subverting those rights that are actually in practice in communities.

In the second place, the English utilitarian philosopher Bentham puts forward both philosophical and political arguments against the premises of French "Declaration of the Rights of Man and the Citizen" in his *Anarchical Fallacies*. He rejects the French Declaration as a body of meaningless statements – "nonsense upon stilts". It makes no sense at all, for him, to talk of abstract rights that existed prior to, or independently of, a system of legal procedure. Politically, on the other hand, he argues that the talk of rights may incite individuals to turn out to be the rebellion of law and government, and thereby creating chaos and disharmony in the state. He objected to the idea of providing a place of them in the national constitutions, for that would "enslave" the future generations to the will of their ancestors.

In the third place, Mary Wollstonecraft (1759-97), a feminist author, develops a scathing attack against the eighteenth-century doctrine of natural rights in her *A Vindication of the Rights of Women* (1792). She criticizes Burke for his support of hereditary rights and of the *status quo* in the social and political life of men. She supports the French Revolution and the subsequent French Declaration, which for the first time propagate the values of liberty, equality and fraternity. But she is critical of the French Revolutionaries for not included women in their conception of men as *rational* creatures. Wollstonecraft argues that women as human beings are rational beings, and it is proper education and training that would enable them to be on the same footing of men. And thereby women, by virtue of possessing "reason", can claim to have their inherent dignity and right, which have so far been ignored by one and all including the so-called revolutionaries.

And in the fourth place, Marx provides a radical critique of the rights of man as part of his general criticism of "bourgeois" society in an essay called "On the Jewish Question" and other writings. Like both Burke and Bentham, Marx rejects the doctrine of the rights of man for its individualistic and abstract character. Human rights, as Marx sees them, belong to individual person who is abstracted from all social relationships or circumstances. In this sense, human rights are "nothing but the rights of the members of civil society, i.e. egoistic man, man separated from other men and the community".[8] Further, in bourgeois society, each isolated individual cannot enjoy freedom as much as he wants but within certain limit set by *other* individuals. Moreover, according to bourgeois conception, the right to equality fails to acknowledge the actual inequalities among the individuals in terms of wealth and power. Above all, the so-called theory of rights presents a total misunderstanding of human nature

---

8 K. Marx, "On the Jewish Question", in Jeremy Waldron (ed.) *"Nonsense upon Stilts"*, London: Methuen, 1987, p. 145.

as selfish and egoistic in character. Despite these criticisms, he is not altogether against any conception of human rights. For him, human emancipation lies not in man's abstract nature but in his participation in productive life of society, and thereby ushering in a communist era.

The Idea of Human Rights: Some Contemporary Developments

The philosopher who first made an attempt to develop a theory of rights independently of the natural rights paradigm was T.H. Green (1836-82). He formulates his theory of rights in his *Lectures on the Principles of Political Obligation*, which were first delivered in 1879 at Oxford. He belongs to the leading figure of the idealist school of Oxford and differs from the utilitarian doctrine on many issues, such as human nature, morality and role of the state in human affairs. He, however, believed in the primacy of the individual liberty along with the utilitarians. But his method and approach to the issue were different from them. He had profound belief in the worth and dignity of man, which he received from Kant. For him, it is to protect the dignity of man that rights are needed to be invoked in the social life of man rather than in his individual life, provided each member recognizes in the common good an ideal good for himself as well. Rights, for Green, are fundamentally a combination of claim made by the individual, on the one hand and conceded by the members of the society on the other.

Later, D.G. Ritchie (1853-93) develops a critique of natural rights along with a positive view of his own in his *Natural Rights* (1892). He right away rejects the law of nature as the foundation of rights, for he faces difficulty as to how to interpret the "voice" of nature. According to him, the law of nature admits of no analysis by rational means. He finds the basis of rights on the social utility which does not mean having rights and institutions that are conducive to general happiness as the classical utilitarian philosophers propose but does mean having those fundamental rights that are relevant to certain stage of social development to prevent the society from disintegration. As society is taken by Ritchie to be always moving forward and elevating itself to the next stage of development, the old set of rights loses its validity, and the need for the new set of rights is felt. Thus rights are decided in varying stages of social development on the basis of rational interpretation of experience.

After a long gap of nearly sixty years, human rights again came to occupy the foreground of both philosophical and political debate with the promulgation of UN Declaration of Human Rights, 1948. This document incorporates in it a wide range of human rights beginning with traditionally recognized rights having some characteristic features of Lockean ideas of rights. In this document, the term "natural rights" is replaced by "human rights", and thereby denying "nature" as the foundation of rights. That is, it sets aside the arguments of natural rights thinkers as the philosophical foundation of rights. But it provides no alternative philosophical basis of rights as its objective was to be agreed merely upon *norms*, and not necessarily upon uniformly agreed values and beliefs. Following the adoption of the Universal Declaration of Human Rights by the United Nations, the philosophers and thinkers resume inventing newer dimensions of the notion of human rights, and in the process a vast body of literature on the philosophy of human rights has proliferated till the present day. The chief impetus has come from the intense shock and horror of the Second World War. In the remainder of the chapter we would briefly state some of the philosophical arguments developed during the later half of the twentieth century.

In the first place, Margaret MacDonald published an article, "Natural Rights" (1949), where she dismissed the law of nature as the standard of what ought to be along with the claim that this standard is known by reason which is considered to be the intrinsic property of man in the natural rights tradition. She argues that man's ability to reason is simply an empirical fact, which does not constitute his specific nature, and hence cannot set the standard of what ought to be. For her, assertions concerning natural law and natural rights are ethical assertions which cannot be known by reason but can only be defended in a manner that a lawyer defends his client. In the second place, Carl Wellman applies Hohfeld's model of legal rights to understand human rights in his article, "A New Conception of Human Rights" (1978). He adopts Hohfeld's conception of legal rights as a "cluster of legal liberties, claims, powers and immunities" as his model and develops an analogous conception of ethical rights as a cluster of ethical liberties, claims, powers and immunities. In the third place, Joel Feinberg in his paper, "The Nature and Value of Rights" (1970), argues that rights consist of making a claim to something and against someone the recognition of which is called for not necessarily by legal rules but by moral principles. In the fourth place, Rex Martin argues in his article, "Human Rights and Civil Rights" (1980), that a moral claim can be considered as valid but it requires appropriate practices, recognition and promotion in order to qualify it as a human right. In the fifth place, David Lyons in his article, "Human Rights and the General Welfare" (1977), makes an attempt to repudiate the presumption that a commitment to the utilitarian belief that moral norms are justified when they are committed to serve the welfare of the society is in conflict with the belief in rights and justice. And he explores the connection between human rights and general welfare by his close reading of famous utilitarian philosopher J.S. Mill. Besides, there are a number of thinkers, such as Ronald Dworkin, Joseph Raz, Maurice Cranston, Henry Shue, Alan Gewirth, and H.L.A. Hart, who have dealt with various aspects and made major contributions to the contemporary understanding of human rights.

Conclusion

Though the term "human rights" is of recent origin, its historical roots can be traced back to Greek and medieval thoughts. This idea that there is a law higher than any human authority, governing the affairs of men, began to dominate from antiquity to the medieval period. The idea of natural law finds its expression in the writings of Sophocles, Aristotle, Epictectus, Cicero, Thomas Aquinas, Hugo Grotius and others. They gave differing interpretations of the idea of natural law from which the idea of natural rights originated in the seventeenth century. Thus the idea of natural rights was an outgrowth of the idea of the natural law. This idea of natural rights was developed into a theoretical structure at the hands of the European Enlightenment thinkers, such as Hobbes, Locke and Paine. But the popularity of the idea of natural rights began to decline when Bentham, Burke and Marx developed their scathing attack on it. Towards the later half of the nineteenth century, many thinkers began to develop the idea of rights independently of the natural rights paradigm. Among these thinkers include Green, Ritchie, MacDonald, Wellman, Feinberg, Martin, Lyons and many others.

3

Rights as Natural Endowment
Some Philosophical Theories

In order to have a systematic understanding of human rights it is worthwhile to begin with an analysis of early modern theories of rights, which constitute the natural rights tradition. Although the origins of the idea of natural rights lie in ancient Greek and medieval philosophies it is customary to begin with Hobbes's analysis of rights, which is regarded as the first *modern* version given as part of a political theory. The latter is joined some forty years later by John Locke whose arguments for natural rights have been more clear and elegant than those of the other philosophers in the tradition. And Thomas Paine restated the Lockean idea of natural rights in his own way in the context of the rebuttal of Burke's view on the subject after hundred years later. The contribution of these three philosophers lays the foundation of today's rights-discourse. Therefore it is of profound importance to delineate and reflect on these philosophical theories of rights in order to understand the later developments on the subject.

Thomas Hobbes: Setting the Stage for Modern Rights-debates

Hobbes' notion of natural rights is inextricably bound up with his conception of the "state of nature". This state is "the natural condition of mankind", i.e. the condition which men are naturally in, in contrast to his artificial condition under a political system. Hobbes conceives the way in which men, being what they are, would necessarily behave by depicting the state of nature where there is no authority to enforce contract or law. The state of nature is interpreted as "a logical hypothesis",[1] rather than a historical hypothesis. That is, it is a condition of men which is logically prior to the formation of a sovereign and historically, there was nothing like the state of nature. In the state of nature, man is believed to have lived by himself with no common superior on earth to subjugate him or his fellow-beings. As men lived "without a common power to keep them all in awe", the condition of human life was a state of war. Man in the state of nature as depicted by Hobbes was deprived of all benefits of civilization: no industry, no culture of the earth, no arts, no machines, no navigation, no geography and no society. In this condition, man lived in "continual fear and danger of violent death; and the life of man [was] solitary, poor, nasty, brutish and short".[2]

This human predicament in the state of nature, according to Hobbes, lies neither with sin nor with depravity but with human nature itself. He discovers man as the creature of desires and passions, always aspiring for pleasure and avoiding pain. The object which maximizes pleasure is one that for which he hankers after rather than pleasure itself. Like Bentham according to whom man is pleasure-seeking being, Hobbesian man seeks not pleasure but the object which brings with it the pleasure. It is the object that rouses pleasure in man through sensation. So Hobbes's moral psychology seems to be based on stimulus–response and not on pleasure–pain considerations like the utilitarians. Further, Hobbes views man as egoistic and ego-centric being, who is always in motion to satisfy his

---

1 C.B. Macpherson, *The Political Theory of Possessive Individualism: Hobbes to Locke,* Oxford: Oxford University Press, 1962, p. 21.

2 T. Hobbes, *Leviathan* (ed.), with an Introduction and Notes by J.C.A. Gaskin, Oxford: Oxford University Press, Oxford World's Classics, 2008, p. 84.

appetites. Though he constantly strives to satisfy his appetites, the latter remain insatiable. For, the satisfaction of one appetite gives rise to the others. Appetites recur in man again and again in course of time. For Hobbes, man is also a rational creature but his reason or rationality is subordinate to his desires and passions. That is to say, a man is always driven by his desires and passions, and goes so far as to quarrel with his fellow-beings to satisfy them, despite the presence of rationality in him. Furthermore, Hobbes discovers in man three principal causes of conflict: competition, diffidence and glory. That is to say, man competes with one another for satisfying his appetites and passions; he lacks self-reliance and is always alert to his self-defence; and he reacts violently if he is undervalued directly or indirectly by his fellow beings. Thus man in the state of nature leads a life of suspicion and rivalry with one another to attain his desired goals in life. Moreover, Hobbes' natural man is not only asocial but amoral as well, for he is unable to discern the distinction between justice and injustice, right and wrong. In this state,

> The notions of right and wrong, justice and injustice have there no place. Where there is no common power, there is no law: where no law, no injustice. Force, and fraud, are in war the two cardinal virtues.[3]

Therefore, the melancholy and chaotic state of nature follows from the consideration of man's predominantly appetitive and passionate nature. It is in each individual's interest that the human appetites and passions are needed to be ruled, and their consequent behaviour is to be co-ordinated and thereby the anarchy of the state of nature is to be replaced by *order*. Now the question is: what place do the natural rights occupy in this scenario? Says Hobbes:

---

[3] T. Hobbes, *Leviathan*, p. 85.

> The Right of Nature, which writers commonly call *jus naturale,* is the liberty each man hath, to use his own power, as he will himself, for the preservation of his own nature; that is to say, of his own life; and consequently, of doing any thing, which in his own judgement, and reason, he shall conceive to be the aptest means thereunto.[4]

In this definition, Hobbes indicates several features that characterize his conception of rights. First, there is only *one* right of nature – the right of self-preservation which one possesses in the state of nature. The term "self-preservation" here means the defense of oneself in psycho-physical terms. The psycho-physical existence of man is taken to be something of value, and the preservation of oneself as valuable object is the sole right of nature. Second, the self-preservation as the natural rights is tied to the individual person. That is, this right is enjoyed by the individual. Third, the liberty to use his own power to self-preservation, according to Hobbes, is the right of nature which each man possesses in the state of nature. That is, each man is at liberty to use his power or to pursue *anything* to preserve his own life as his judgement and reason dictate him to do. Hobbes is in favour of unlimited exercise of will to preserve one's life. However, the right of nature that ordains him to defend his own life is only an effort towards its preservation and does *not* ensure its preservation. As F.C. Hood rightly says:

> This is no more than a right of endeavour. There is no right of achievement; and in this sense there is no natural right to life or to anything else. In fleeing from an enemy, a man may fail to jump over a ditch, and must fail to jump over the moon. If he attempts the impossible – and no man will attempt what he knows to be impossible – he errs, but he does not exceed his right of nature. No law of nature in

---

4 T. Hobbes, *Leviathan,* p. 86.

> Hobbes sense forbids a man to attempt to jump over the moon. It is needless for law to prohibit an impossible action.[5]

Fourth, in one's unlimited exercise of will and in having any recourse to secure his life, he need not recognize the same right of other individuals. As for Hobbes, a right implies *no* duty towards others. For him, right of nature implies absence of duty. And thus a right has its unlimited expansion in a regime of *no* duty towards other individuals.

The right of nature, for Hobbes, has two dimensions:

1. A man originally possesses the natural right to everything for his self-preservation in the state of nature. He retains this right even after the institution of a government, though its sphere is reduced to a minimum. That is, he holds the right only against the government in case he is threatened by it, despite he unconditionally agree to obey one supreme authority like the government. For example, if the government orders a man to kill his fellow-being, then the latter may resist this threat by virtue of possessing the right of nature. In this sense, the right of nature is inalienable.
2. Another dimension is that the right of every man to everything must be given up as a necessary condition for the institution of a sovereign in order to put an end to the anarchy of the state of nature. This is "the Right of Governing my Selfe" which is unconditionally handed over to the sovereign along with the right of everyone else. The unconditional obedience to the sovereign allows the latter to co-ordinate the behaviour of its subjects and to maintain the common standard of justice and injustice.

---

[5] F.C. Hood, *The Divine Politics of Thomas Hobbes: An Interpretation of Leviathan*, Oxford: Clarendon Press, 1964, p. 90.

Though right and law are closely associated, in the sense that the former becomes meaningful only in relation to the latter, Hobbes insists that they "ought" to be distinguished. He writes:

> A Law of Nature (*lex naturalis*) is a precept, or general rule, found out by reason, by which a man is forbidden to do, that, which is destructive of his life, or taketh away the means of preserving the same; and to omit, that, by which he thinketh it may be best preserved. For though they that speak of this subject, use to confound *jus*, and *lex*, *right* and *law*; yet they ought to be distinguished; because RIGHT, consisteth in liberty to do, or to forbear: whereas LAW, determineth, and bindeth to one of them, so that law, and right, differ as much, as obligation, and liberty; which in one and the same matter are inconsistent.[6]

Let us analyse the distinction between right and law following Hobbes. Right, according to him, consists in liberty to or abstain from doing anything for his own preservation, and law is that which forbids doing anything that destroys his life and takes away the means of its preservation. In other words, to have a right implies that one is free to take a decision on any particular occasion whether or not to do, or to claim that which the right entitles him to do. There is an element of freedom to act on one's *own* judgement and responsibility in right, which is absent in a law or obligation. To act in accordance with a law or under an obligation, one is *not* free to take a decision whether or not he will do it. A law puts restraint upon the individual, and regulates his conduct. But if this discretion of the individual is not there in a right, then there would remain no liberty to forego it if and when he finds it convenient to relinquish. The right of nature, on the one hand, entitles a person to take possession of everything,

[6] T. Hobbes, *Leviathan*, p. 86.

and this may lead him to involve himself in war with others. But the law of nature, on the other, ordains him to renounce some portions of what he is entitled to claim for the enjoyment of others, and this renunciation or transfer of rights leads to the avoidance of war and establishment of peace. For Hobbes, the right of nature is not a *moral* right but the power to claim each and everything with *no* regard for others' similar claims. It must be noted that Hobbes' definition of right is subjective in character, in the sense that it is prompted by each man's desire for peace and the fear of death, and it finds expression in the power and liberty to do anything that leads to his own preservation.

An important point that merits attention here is: On the one hand, what Hobbes calls "the right of nature" prescribes man to have the liberty to do anything that leads him to preserve his own life, i.e. he has discretion or liberty as to whether or not he will discharge it. On the other, in accordance with the law of nature, one is under an obligation to do anything to preserve his life, which implies that he is not free to choose whether or not he will do it. According to this view, it follows that one cannot have both a right and a law to the same thing. That is, one makes the other impossible.[7]

---

[7] As Richard Tuck clarifies, "The thing which Hobbes was interested in, and which made this a *right* or a *liberty* and not a duty, was that in nature we are each to do what *we* want in order to preserve ourselves. It is this open-endedness, this dependence solely upon the will of the individual agent, which is important about a right, and it was this which Hobbes captured by describing our natural capacity to make our own decisions about how to protect ourselves as a right. The 'law' of nature tells us what we *ought* to decide if we are thinking rationally, but the 'right' tells us that it is we who have to decide, and that we are naturally and psychologically free to go any way we choose towards the necessary goal of our survival". See Tuck's *Hobbes: A Very Short Introduction*, Oxford: Oxford University Press, 2002, p. 73.

Notice here the following two points that differentiate Hobbes' distinction between right and law from the traditional view on the matter:

1. In the first place, Hobbes' distinction between law and right runs counter to the traditional understanding of the relationship between the two. From the traditional point of view, on the one hand, the natural law flows from the *rational* human nature and includes both individual and social virtues, which helps man in his ethical development. On the other hand, the natural right is a derivative of *social* human nature and thus originates in social relations; it includes only social virtues, such as justice and benevolence. Consequently, in traditional understanding of the matter, the natural right has a narrower connotation than that of natural law. Thus the natural rights originate from the natural law. Hobbes, on the contrary, holds that the law of nature owes it origin in the right of nature, and the former is needed to protect the latter.
2. In the second place, traditionally the laws of a civil government find their *moral* basis in the law of nature that had been prevailing in the state of nature. For, the law of nature is something that flows from human nature itself, and thus it is an eternal law. Therefore, it is not man-made and subject to *no* change or mutation like positive laws. But for Hobbes, on the contrary, the civil law is the source of the law of nature which regulates people to behave socially and morally. In other words, it is the civil laws that bind people to be social and moral. According to Hobbes, morality does not flow from human nature but from civil government.

Let us now turn to Hobbes' conception of liberty and see what role it plays in his scheme of rights. "By LIBERTY", he writes,

> is understood, according to the proper signification of the word, the absence of external impediments: which impediments, may oft take away part of a man's power to do what he would; but cannot hinder him from using the power left him, according as his judgement, and reason shall dictate to him.[8]

According to this definition, you have the liberty to use your power to preserve your life to the extent that no external hindrances stand in the way to do so. But liberty, in this sense, does not coincide with what is meant by right. Right, for Hobbes, means the liberty to do or to forbear, and it tells us that it is you who have to decide and you are free to take any means towards the necessary goal of your survival. The role of Hobbes' conception of liberty in his theory of rights is this: The law of nature ordains that you must use your power to preserve your life, and the law of nature tells this in its status as a "rule of reason". That is, if you rationally think, then you *ought* to decide the means as to how you protect your life. But, according to Hobbes's view of liberty, you are free to disobey the rule of reason (i.e. the law of nature) as there is no external hindrance in the way. Thus when the law of nature tells you that you ought to preserve your life, then this does not do away with the existence of your right of nature to preserve your life.

John Locke: Rights as Centre-piece of Political Thought

Locke's view on natural rights is considered to be the most influential of the modern versions on the subject. In his analysis of rights, he sticks more to the traditionalism than Hobbes's view of it in that the law of nature or the natural law is regarded by him as God's design for men quite in line with the view of medieval scholastic philosophers, such as Thomas

[8] T. Hobbes, *Leviathan*, p. 86.

Aquinas. Yet his view concurs as well, in some important respects, with the Enlightenment and liberal thinking on the subject.

According to Locke, men fundamentally belong to the state of nature where they enjoy perfect freedom and equality in the absence of a government. He discovers in men a sense of sociability, in the sense that they are naturally drawn to families and communities in the state of nature prior to the formation of any government. Locke points out that the state of nature, though unstable, is not a "brutish" condition as it is held by Hobbes. In it, all men stand on equal footing in respect of rationality, freedom of action and the equality of opportunity. It is rationality or reason which differentiates men from all other species on earth and enables them to play their part in God's design for the world. Further, men are provided with freedom of choice. Freedom consists in taking a decision in favour or disfavour of their proposal and converts it into an action. Moreover, the state of nature is also a state of equality, in the sense that they are provided with all the same advantages of nature; they are all members of the same species; and they possess the same cognitive faculties and emotions. Each and every person resides in the state of nature on equal standing without subordination or subjection. But it is to be noted that despite his possession of rationality, freedom of choice and the equality, he is still, according to Locke, serving the purpose of God. What is man's duty to God becomes a right against other men in Locke's philosophy of rights.

Thus man used to enjoy rights in the state of nature prior to social contract and hence before the appearance of a government. It is the responsibility of the sovereign and its legitimate political institutions to accommodate these rights. For Hobbes, rights do not exist before the formation of a government; rather, they follow from it. But, for Locke, rights are coeval with man in the state of nature and continue to exist *inalienably* with the patronage of the state. Just as rights are held back in the state of nature by man, so is man insulated from the intrusion of his private space by the state or other agencies after the establishment of a government. For Hobbes, rights are *theorems*, but for Locke, they are *premises*.[9]

The point that needs to be emphasized is that the freedom given to men by God is not a state of licence to do as he likes. This freedom is "within the bounds of the law of nature" as the state of nature is governed by the law of nature. Locke writes:

> The state of nature has a law of nature to govern it, which obliges everyone: and reason, which is that law, teaches all mankind, who will but consult it, that being all equal and independent, no one ought to harm another in his life, health, liberty, or possessions.[10]

The natural law, according to Locke, is the supreme law of morality, and everyone ought to observe it. This law can be known by reason. That is, the rational and reflective persons are capable of knowing this law. Human reason, according to Locke, stands for logical reason which distinguishes him from "brute beasts" as well as enables him to perceive what is right and wrong, liberty and equality, law and obligation. The natural law, as the law of reason, guides him to his general good, i.e., to protect his life, liberty and possessions. That is to say, every man is entitled by this law to preserve his life, to have his freedom of action and to use his property as he thinks fit, provided that he does not stand in the way of any other man's enjoyment of the same condition. Thus Locke derives

---

9 A. Levine, *Engaging Political Philosophy: From Hobbes to Rawls*, Oxford: Blackwell Publishers, 2002, p. 97.

10 J. Locke, (ed.) *Two Treatises of Government*, with an Introduction by Mark Goldie, London: Everyman, 1993, p. 117.

his concept of natural rights from the law of nature. It is "reason, which is that law" that sets up the rights and the corresponding duties or obligations. Let us consider Locke's right to life, liberty and property taking one at a time.

THE RIGHT TO LIFE

It is man's first duty to preserve his own life and consequently the means of his subsistence. Though he is entitled to enjoy unrestrained liberty in the state of nature, he is not at liberty to destroy himself. Rather, Locke writes,

> everyone as he is bound to preserve himself, and not to quit his station willfully; so by the like reason when his own preservation comes not in competition, ought he, as much as he can, to preserve the rest of mankind, and may not unless it be to do justice on an offender, take away, or impair the life, or what tends to the preservation of the life, the liberty, health, limb or goods of another.[11]

Locke means to say here that man possesses a property in his own person but the right of this property belongs to God as the creator. As man has an obligation under the law of nature to preserve himself, this law at once *entitles* him to preserve himself. This right to man's preservation of himself presupposes the other man's obligation to respect that right. Thus one's right to life would have no value if the legitimacy of this right is not acknowledged by others. Besides, everyone has the obligation under the law of nature to come to the assistance of others when their preservation is threatened. In order to protect other's life, Locke points out, one need not put his own life at risk. This limit on mutual assistance of protecting one another is one of the defects of the state of nature that invites a political system to be in place for the protection of all.

---

[11] J. Locke, *Two Treatises of Government*, p. 117.

The natural consequence of Locke's natural law theory is that all citizens of the state of nature are entitled, i.e. to have a natural right to judge and punish offenders against the law of nature. Each individual in the state of nature is a competent judge and an executioner of the law of nature. By executing the law of nature, an observer of the natural law puts restraint on the offender's invasion of others' rights; he is entitled to have a natural right to interfere with offender against it to the extent that he deserves to be punished. If nobody in the state of nature possesses the power of executing the law to his own hands, then the law of nature would be useless. As the state of nature is the state of perfect equality and there is no superiority of one over the other, it is necessary to ensure the preservation of the innocents.

What follows is that the violation of the law of nature by an offender disqualifies him to be a peace-loving citizen of the state of nature, and thereby he "becomes dangerous to mankind". In this connection, Locke seems to have identified three purposes of punishment – the retribution, reparation and restraint. In other words, in retribution, the offender is paid back for the harm he has done to the innocent; in reparation, the damage or injury done to the innocent is restituted; and in restraint, the offender as well as potential transgressors of the law of nature is prevented from like offences against the state of nature in view of the punishment.

THE RIGHT TO EQUALITY AND LIBERTY

The state of nature, according to Locke, is a state of equality and liberty. All men living in the state of nature enjoy equal status as members of the human species. No one is superior to the other. There is also no common superior on earth to be ruled by. They are provided with same advantages of nature. They are equal in terms of having reciprocal power and jurisdiction. They are born rational and use the same faculties.

The state of nature is also a state of liberty. The state of nature, Locke writes,

> is a state of perfect freedom to order their actions, and dispose of their possessions, and persons as they think fit, within the bounds of the law of nature, without asking leave, or depending upon the will of any other man.[12]

The use of the phrase, "within the bounds of the law of nature" indicates that the freedom of man in the state of nature is not unbounded but in accordance with the law of nature. Locke seems to have found the limit to man's freedom in the rights of others. But of one thing Locke is certain is that this natural right to freedom does not depend on other's arbitrary will or power but freedom that is permitted by the law of nature. The freedom from absolute and arbitrary power is necessary both for his physical subsistence and for the development of his moral personhood. "Thus we are born free, as we are born rational."[13]

THE RIGHT TO PROPERTY

Let us finally consider Locke's natural right to property. The question that first arises is: what does Locke mean by property? In response to this question, Locke says:

> By property I must be understood here, as in other places, to mean that property which men have in their persons as well as goods.[14]

According to Locke, every person has a right in the state of nature to appropriate the goods of the earth for his self-preservation. The earth together with all it contains is by nature common to all men. The right to own possessions prior to any

---

[12] J. Locke, *Two Treatises of Government*, p. 116.

[13] Ibid., p. 144.

[14] Ibid., p. 204.

civil society and government does not depend on the consent of other persons to it. It is to ensure his self-preservation that the natural right to own property is given to him by God. Locke claims that a person owns a property in the state of nature in whatever he has "mixed his labour with" and thereby attaches to it (i.e. external object) something of his *own*. Locke explains his position as follows:

> Though the earth, and all inferior creatures be common to all men, yet every man has a property in his own person. This nobody has any right to but himself. The labour of his body, and the work of his hands, we may say, are properly his. Whatsoever then he removes out of the state that nature hath provided, and left it in, he hath mixed his labour with, and joined to it something that is his own, and thereby makes it his property. It being by him removed from the common state nature placed it in, it hath by this labour something annexed to it, that excludes the common right of other men. For this labour being the unquestionable property of the labourer, no man but he can have a right to what that is once joined to, at least where there is enough, and as good left in common for others.[15]

What follows is that the property as such is not given to men by the nature but he can reduce an object into a property by his capacity of labour. The latter itself is a kind of property of men from the outset and remains so forever. In order to reduce an external object to *his* property, he is required, according to Locke, to expend his resources and labour to this end. Needless to say, it is his labour that puts value on external objects and makes it *his* own. In other words, the right to own an external object to be *his* property is based only on the labour that he has bestowed upon it, and it is this labour that at once excludes others from the right of the same object.

---

[15] J. Locke, *Two Treatises of Government*, p. 128.

As Locke argues for the right to own property on the basis of one's labour, he seems to have assumed that there is no shortage of land or natural resources on earth at least in the earlier stages of the state of nature. As regards the ownership of property by virtue of labour, Locke issues a caveat. When a person, for example, gathers some fruits from the forest, he no doubt can claim these fruits to be *his* own. But if these fruits are rotted before he could make use of them, then this would go against the law of nature, and the person responsible for the wastage, according to Locke, is liable to be punished. Now the question is: if the state of nature is presumed to be a state of plenty, why this prohibition against waste? Locke seems to have *not* issued this prohibition when there are enough resources for everyone but only when there is a situation of shortage. And in such a situation, there remains the possibility that other people may be deprived. Since, for Locke, under the law of nature we all have duties to save others' lives.

In this connection, another question may arise: why the right to property is recognized by Locke to be a *natural* right? To our understanding, the right to property under civil law can be claimed on the basis that individuals in the state of nature are in possession of land or natural resources *under* the law of nature. Since any property is a means of self-preservation, Locke refers back to the state of nature where under the law of nature he is *entitled* to own a property by the capacity of his labour. That is, Locke seems to have found the *moral* basis of owning a property under civil law in the state of nature. This seems to be the significance of Locke's theory of natural property rights.

Though Locke's portrayal of the state of nature is quite appealing, it is not, according to him, a stable condition of men. In spite of the fact that human beings are born rational, they do *not* always behave in accordance with the rule of reason. Reason sometimes gives way to force and fraud. Driven by their selfish interests, men may become biased instead of acting in accordance with the law of nature or reason. Although people enjoy the natural rights to life, liberty and estate in the state of nature, the latter cannot provide adequate guarantee for the safeguard of property in the general sense of the term. Hence, there arises the question of entering into what Locke calls "compact" with his fellow-beings to form a political system which is supposed to be capable of providing them with adequate guarantee for the protection of lives, liberties and estates. This is made possible, according to Locke, only by the consent of one and all, living in the state of nature. And ultimately they hand over the right of judgement and execution to the government.

Now, if the state of nature cannot provide adequate living condition to men and consequently they would have to opt for civil government, then what is Locke's purpose of depicting the state of nature? Locke seems to have been in search of a *moral* basis of human rights, liberties and possessions, which he has found in the state of nature governed by its own law. The natural rights to life, liberty and estate, as we pointed out earlier, are derivative from the natural law in Locke's philosophy of rights.

Though these rights originate from the state of nature by virtue of the natural law, the state of nature can*not* ensure their execution. The task of maintaining the *status quo* prevailing in the state of nature, according to Locke, is to be entrusted to a civil government. In other words, it is the political society constituted in accordance with the law of nature can only provide guarantee to men for a life that is enjoyed in the state of nature. The state of nature, where the rights of the individual originate, is to be superseded by a political system that is supposed to secure these rights for the individual. The state of nature and its law provide the *moral* basis for the rights that are supposed to be guaranteed and consequently enjoyed by the individuals in a political society. Like Hobbesian right of nature, the Lockean natural rights receive their normative force *not* from the sovereign but from their presence in the state of nature as inalienable rights. Further, though the sovereign is established by "compact" in order to legislate laws and to assign rights, its foremost task is to enforce the natural rights that pre-exist the sovereign. Like Hobbesian sovereign, the Lockean state is not, in the main, a right maker but rather a right enforcer. Locke argues for a minimal government whose basic task is to enforce the natural rights, and it is in its willingness and ability to protect these rights that make its existence meaningful and beneficial for the masses.

Thomas Paine: Restatement of Natural Rights

Paine introduces his theory of natural rights in the context of his rebuttal of Burke's views on the French Revolution in his *The Rights of Man.* In this book Paine first grounded his political theory entirely on the concepts of natural rights and popular sovereignty. Whereas Burke regards the precedent and tradition as the basis of social and political actions, Paine found it necessary to be selective in the choice of precedent and tradition among the many available to base the social and political life. Unlike Burke, he had little reverence for the tradition. As a conservative political thinker, Burke argues for *status quo* but Paine regards human rights that have found expression in the eighteenth-century *Declarations* and *Bills of Rights* to be the basis of making decisions about the social and political life. While laying stress on the natural rights as the basis of social and political life, Paine makes a distinction between society and state – the former being natural and the latter artificial in origin. He writes:

> Some writers have so confounded society with government, as to leave little or no distinction between them; whereas

> they are not only different, but have different origins. Society is produced by our wants and government by our wickedness; the former promotes our happiness *positively* by uniting our affections, the latter *negatively* by restraining our vices. The one encourages intercourse, the other creates distinctions. The first is a patron, the last a punisher.[16]

For him, society is a "blessing" for the people but government even in its best state is but a "necessary evil". He reduces the significance and importance of government to a minimum, and exalts the role of society in peoples' lives. The function of an executive power remains to be limited to the creation of law and the administration of them. For, the policy of political *laissez faire* will pave the way for the enjoyment of rights in society.

In his search for the origin of rights, Paine rejects the arguments from historical precedent. For, the arguments from history do not go back far enough. In order to base the claims about rights, one has to go back all the way and only then "we shall come to the time when man came from the hand of his Maker".[17] That is, he found the basis of rights on accounts of the creation. And accordingly, for him, the rights of man are divine in origin; the divine creation is the sole authority of the rights of man. This authority simply confirms what Paine calls *"the unity of man"*, i.e. the principle that

> men are all of *one degree*, and consequently that all men are born equal, and with equal natural rights, in the same manner as if posterity had been continued by *creation* instead of *generation*, the latter being only the mode by which the former is carried forward; and consequently every child born into the world must be considered as deriving its existence from God.[18]

---

16 T. Paine, "Common Sense", in John Dos Passos (ed.) *The Living Thoughts of Tom Paine,* New Delhi: Rupa & Co., 2002, p. 64.

17 T. Paine, *The Rights of Man*, London: Everyman, 1966, p. 41.

18 Ibid., p. 42.

This idea of equality of man is grounded by Paine on his deistic belief in a Supreme Being. For, men are equal in worth and value in the eyes of God.

Paine's view on the rights of man is based on the Lockean premises and Enlightenment ideas that have found expression in eighteenth-century *Declarations* and *Bills of Rights*. Though Paine claims to have not read Locke, but he is influenced by the latter. For, at that time, the British political institutions were permeated by the Lockean thoughts and ideas. So Paine could not keep himself free of Lockean influences. Like Locke, Paine insists on the complete equality of all individuals. He also includes the Lockean right to liberty, property and security, as well as the derivative right of resistance to oppression in his list of rights. But there are points of difference between Locke and Paine. Locke is in favour of putting restrictions on the religious freedom of individuals in order to maintain peace and harmony in society, whereas Paine argues against the exercise of state's power over individual's religious beliefs. Further, unlike Locke, for whom a government is contract or a "compact" between rulers and governed, Paine thinks government to be a contract between sovereign individuals who uniformly decide to subordinate some of their individual rights to social order. On Paine's view, a government is a contract among *equals*. Thus Paine writes:

> The fact therefore must be that the *individuals themselves*, each in his own personal and sovereign right, *entered into a compact with each other* to produce a Government: and this is the only mode in which Governments have a right to arise and the only principle on which they have a right to exist.[19]

But men do not have to surrender their natural rights upon entering a political society. Some of the natural rights are retained by the individual, and some of them are sacrificed or

---

[19] T. Paine, *The Rights of Man*, p. 47.

rather exchanged by him in favour of the formation of a social order – the latter being the civil rights. The former rights are personal in nature and belong to him as an individual. But what he calls "civil rights" are enjoyed by him only as a member of society. Paine makes a conceptual distinction between "natural rights" and "civil rights" as follows:

> Natural rights are those which appertain to man in right of his existence. Of this kind are all the intellectual rights, or rights of the mind, and also all those rights of acting as an individual for his own comfort and happiness, which are not injurious to the natural rights of others. Civil rights are those which appertain to man in right of his being a member of society.[20]

The natural rights that are retained by the individual are rights whose power and authority of execution lie with the individual alone. Society cannot have jurisdiction over these rights. In exercizing these rights, individual needs *no* assistance from the civil society and government. Among the rights that are retained by the individual are all intellectual rights, the freedom of religious choice, and freedom of expression in its various forms. But the civil rights, on the contrary, cannot be retained by the individual but is exchanged in favour of the formation of a social order. The power to execute them does not lie with the individual. That is, his individual power is not sufficiently competent in all cases to safeguard these rights. It is the civil power, that is, the collective support of civil society and government that is capable of executing these rights for individuals living in society. Paine writes:

> *That civil power properly considered as such is made up of the aggregate of that class of the natural rights of man, which becomes defective in the individual in point of power, and answers not his*

---

20 T. Paine, *The Rights of Man*, p. 44.

> *purpose, but when collected to a focus becomes competent to the purpose of everyone.*[21]

These rights include the right to security and protection. Thus in order to live in society, individual has to exchange some of his natural rights for civil rights. But the point to be noted is that the natural rights are the foundations of civil rights. As Paine says,

> A man, by natural right, has a right to judge in his own cause; and so far as the right of the mind is concerned, he never surrenders it. But what availeth it him to judge, if he has not power to redress? He therefore deposits this right in the common stock of society and takes the arm of society, of which he is a part, in preference and in addition to his own. Society *grants* him nothing. Every man is a proprietor in society and draws on the capital as a matter of right.[22]

In order to live a dignified life in society with all his rights protected, an individual comes to an agreement with his fellow-men. By nature, an individual has the right to protect his own person and to have him secured. But he does not possess sufficient power in himself for his own protection. If he is left to himself, he cannot protect himself, and so he is obliged to seek assistance and relief of his fellow-men.[23] In order to obtain what is rightfully his own, he joins hands with his fellow men and thereby enter into a social contract or "compact" in order to make the everyday living possible. The purpose of

---

21 T. Paine, *The Rights of Man*, p. 45 (emphasis original).

22 Ibid.

23 In order to make clear the desirability of society than a government, Paine writes the following: "In this state of natural liberty, society will be their first thought. A thousand motives will excite them thereto; the strength of one man is so unequal to his wants, and his mind so unfitted for perpetual solitude, that he is soon obliged to seek assistance and relief of another, who in his turn requires the same." See his "Common Sense", in *The Living Thoughts of Tom Paine*, p. 65.

government or any executive power is to ensure the enjoyment of the civil rights. For,

> Man did not enter into society to become *worse* than he was before, nor to have fewer rights than he had before, but to have those rights better secured. His natural rights are the foundation of all his civil rights.[24]

The natural rights that are enjoyed by the individuals upon their entering a society are not granted by the government. Government grants him nothing. The latter acts only as the guarantor of rights which are already possessed by the individual. The sole task of government is to maintain law and order among the citizens and to protect individual rights, so that each citizen may lead a life with a maximum of security, freedom and equality. It is in order to secure these civil rights that individuals as equals agree to form a nation in which people as a whole are sovereign. In this social compact, right and power are supposed to be equivalent and accepted by each person. The sole purpose of social compact is mutual protection and benefit in terms of rights. In this context, Mark Philp notes:

> In its essentials this account is similar to that of Locke, who also saw the function of society in terms of more perfectly securing our natural rights. Although Paine's case is less sharply formulated than Locke's, its basic claim is unmistakable. Civil rights remain rooted in natural rights; together, the two kinds provide the indefeasible framework within which legitimate civil authorities must operate. This is why he includes both natural and civil rights when discussing declarations of the rights of man. The social compact must guarantee protection for both types of natural rights.[25]

---

[24] T. Paine, *The Rights of Man*, p. 44.

[25] M. Philp, *Paine*, Oxford: Oxford University Press, 1989, p. 60.

As Paine follows the French "Declaration of the Rights of Man and the Citizen" in formulating his views on rights, he quotes the first three of the seventeen articles that define the ambit of rights for him, in *The Rights of Man*. These are:

I. Men are born, and always continue, free and equal in respect of their rights. Civil distinctions, therefore, can be founded only on public utility.

II. The end of all political associations is the preservation of the natural and imprescriptible rights of man; and these rights are liberty, property, security and resistance of oppression.

III. The Nation is essentially the source of all sovereignty; nor can *Any Individual*, or *Any Body of Men*, be entitled to any authority which is not expressly derived from it.[26]

In his attempt to refute Burke's views on the French Revolution and related issues in *The Rights of Man*, Paine's attention has remained focused throughout on the issue of natural and civil rights. This would be clearer from the following observations. In the first place, Paine rejects monarchical and hereditary form of government where social compact means contract of submission to a ruler. The hereditary government often becomes autocratic and does not take care of the rights of its subjects. The ruler may suspend people's natural rights at his will at any time. So Paine prefers to have a contract of association among *equals* for the mutual protection of natural rights of its members. In the second place, he minimizes the role and importance of government by limiting its activities only to legislation and administration. Here, Paine is in favour of least possible interference in the natural course of society, and *this* is only to pave the way for the civil rights to remain secured. In the third place, Paine

---

[26] T. Paine, *The Rights of Man*, p. 135.

allows people to gather together to have a government and to draw up a constitution which would provide the framework and principle to function in such a way as to guarantee all natural rights to the people as a whole. And at last, the constitution and government stand for the expression of sovereign will, where each person will have a say in the collective affairs of the nation. The majority voice would be the expression of the will of the nation. But the scope of the government, according to Paine, is delimited by its purpose for which it is brought into existence, that is, to defend the natural and civil rights of all its members.

Conclusion

In the present chapter, an attempt has been made to present the main issues on rights contained in what is known as the natural-rights tradition. First, as the inaugurator of the latter tradition, Hobbes is credited with initiating the modern debates on rights. But he seems to have given a weak rational basis for the idea of "a right of nature". For, he argues that each man must give up his right of nature in favour of the establishment of a government and thereby putting an end to the anarchy of the state of nature. Though each man generally instinctively pursues his self-preservation, his rational nature also tells him to pursue the same. That is, the law of nature, which is a "rule of reason", ordains that each man must give up his right of nature in favour of the institution of a political authority. It is only towards his rational pursuit of self-preservation that he must give up his right of nature in order to pave the way for a government which would be instituted in accordance with the law of nature – the latter being the "precept or general rule found out by reason" that states the condition of rational self-preservation. Thus it is the notion of the law of nature and not the notion of the right of nature that is of central importance in Hobbes's theory of rights.

Second, Locke's conception of rights is considered to be the most clear and prominent among the views put forward by other thinkers in the tradition. He depicts the state of nature where all men stand on equal footing in respect of rationality, freedom of action and the equality of opportunity. In order to maintain the *status quo*, he argues, there arises the need to institute a civil government. He pleads for a *minimal* government the only role of which would be to protect and secure the rights of man, such as the right to life, liberty and possessions.

Third, Paine is greatly influenced by his predecessors in the natural-rights tradition, particularly by Locke as also by enlightenment rationalism in formulating his theory of rights. Accordingly, he sees man as a rational creature, and this rationality of man, according to him, is not acquired by education but something *inherent* in his nature. Thus Paine believes in fixed human nature and locates the source of rights in it, like other natural rights thinkers. Further, he had firm faith on rational and enlightened human beings who would be able to perceive the conveniences of social order and would accept the legitimacy of curtailing individual, in favour of civil, rights. Furthermore, though Paine's writings exhibit a measure of social outlook, yet in ultimate analysis he remains to be an ardent individualist quite in keeping with other natural rights thinkers. Moreover, he is regarded to be more as a staunch defender of rights than as a serious originator of new ideas as he shares many of the issues with other thinkers of the natural rights tradition.

4

The Natural Rights Paradigm
Some Critical Responses

THE natural rights paradigm of what we today call "human rights" has exerted a great influence upon the French Revolution. The basic principles of the doctrine of natural rights had been incorporated in the French "Declaration of the Rights of Man and the Citizen" of 1789. Despite the profound impact of the doctrine of natural rights on the French Revolution it began to provoke critical responses from various perspectives by the end of the eighteenth century. Among those who contributed to this process of critical reactions are Bentham, Burke and Marx. First, Bentham is known as the principal architect of utilitarianism as a central philosophical doctrine. He applies the utilitarian principle to a great variety of political, legal and other perennial issues of mankind. He develops a distinctive utilitarian perspective to evaluate laws, politics and social institutions in his *An Introduction to the Principles of Morals and Legislation*, first published in 1789. But a comprehensive critique of the ideas of natural law and natural rights can be found in a work that was published after his death under the title *Anarchical Fallacies* in the form of a response to the French "Declaration of the Rights of Man and the Citizen".

Second, the principles that were embodied in Locke's theory of natural rights a century ago greatly inspired the French Revolution of 1789 and had immediately been incorporated in the French "Declaration of the Rights of Man and the Citizen". The latter document affirmed the natural rights of Lockean origin as the basis of social and political life. It is against the French Revolution and subsequently adopted *Declaration* to which Burke expresses his reaction in his highly influential work, *Reflections on the Revolution in France,* first published in 1790.

Third, Marx puts forward his criticism of natural rights notably in the context of his examination of Jewish claims to emancipation in Europe. While scrutinizing the French Revolutionary Declaration and Constitution, he clarifies his position with regard to natural rights in "On the Jewish Question" in keeping with his critique of capitalist society. In this chapter we propose to explicate and reflect on these criticisms of natural rights doctrine along with critical reactions given by Ritchie and MacDonald.

Jeremy Bentham: Natural Rights as "Nonsense upon Stilts"

Bentham was a legal positivist, and he uniformly maintained an antagonistic attitude towards the idea of Nature as the source of law and morality. Bentham calls it "the arbitrary principle" or "the principle of sympathy and antipathy".[1] He ridicules Nature by mentioning her as the "goddess"[2] of French revolutionaries. He refers to the rights of man that are derivative of the law of nature as the "pretended rights".[3] Bentham rejects the law of nature as the standard of morality in his *An Introduction to the Principles* of *Morals and Legislation.* He writes:

---

1 J. Bentham, *A Fragment on Government and An Introduction to the Principles of Morals and Legislation,* Wilfred Harrison (ed.), Oxford: Basil Blackwell, 1948, pp. 138-39.

2 J. Bentham, "Anarchical Fallacies" in Jeremy Waldron (ed.) *"Nonsense upon Stilts",* London: Methuen, 1987, p. 55.

3 Ibid.

> A great multitude of people are continually talking of the Law of Nature; and then they go on giving you their sentiments about what is right and what is wrong: and these sentiments, you are to understand, are so many chapters and sections of the Law of Nature.[4]

Bentham replaces the law of nature with the principle of utility, which provides an objective moral standard to judge human actions. For him, moral standard or law does not originate in Nature but in human subject. Human being is the source and legislator of law. Contrary to the proponents of natural rights, Bentham takes away the power of legislation from Nature and transfers it to the rational and autonomous human subject. Now, human legislator, not Nature, would create and promulgate law in accordance with the varied and ephemeral circumstances of the society. Thus Bentham creates a chasm between law and Nature. And thereby he makes an attempt to free humanity from the authority and dictates of the natural law.

Bentham's principal doctrine, namely, utilitarianism has absolutely nothing to do with his critique of natural rights. He writes:

> I know of no natural rights except what are created by general utility: and even in that sense it were much better the word were never heard of. All such language is at any rate false: all such language is either pernicious, or at the best an improper and fallacious way of indicating what is true.[5]

The notion of a right bears significance, according to Bentham, only in the context of law that is made to serve the one and only one utilitarian purpose, i.e. to promote happiness to the

---

[4] J. Bentham, *A Fragment on Government and An Introduction to the Principles of Morals and Legislation*, chapter II, footnotes, p. 141.

[5] J. Bentham, "Supply Without Burthen or Escheat *Vice* Taxation" in *"Nonsense upon Stilts"*, p. 72.

community. The point that Bentham needs stressing here is that all rights are legal, created either by the silence of the law or by prohibition of influence in the exercise of an authority. Law has to be systematic and logical, and to be based on the principle of utility.

Bentham has carried out his scathing attack on the notions of natural law and natural rights as they have been promulgated in the French *Declaration* at a time when the staunch defenders like Thomas Paine, imbued with the Enlightenment spirit, were dilating on these notions. He right away declares:

> *Natural rights* are simple nonsense: natural and imprescriptible rights, rhetorical nonsense – nonsense upon stilts. But this rhetorical nonsense ends in the old strain of mischievous nonsense: for immediately a list of these pretended natural rights is given, and those are so expressed as to present to view legal rights.[6]

This passage indicates the direction of his entire philosophical arguments that Bentham puts forward against the notion of natural rights as enunciated in the *Declaration*. He finds the idea of natural rights as literally nonsense, and that is for two reasons: In the first place, to talk of natural rights, for Bentham, is to talk of something that is devoid of meaning. Some writers have pointed out that his dismissal of natural rights as nonsense is similar to the arguments of the members of the Vienna Circle who later to characterize the propositions of theology and metaphysics as meaningless. In the second place, he shows series of contradictions in the statements of the *Declaration* by citing them in his own writings. This apart, he also elaborates his arguments to lay bare what he calls the "mischievous" character of the notion of rights. Let us turn to analyse these three points of criticism mentioned above.

---

[6] J. Bentham, "Anarchical Fallacies" in *"Nonsense upon Stilts"*, p. 53.

First, Bentham argues that the talk of rights as existing before the establishment of a political system is to talk nonsense. For, the statement of rights in legal sense can be verified, but the statement about rights as said to be originating from Nature and existing independently of the law of any government cannot be so verified. The terms "right" and "duty" make no sense at all outside legal framework, and hence, they are "fictitious" terms. On the contrary, "law", "sovereign" and "sanction" refer to something tangible and can be identified. "Right" and "duty" become intelligible only if they are considered in terms of law or legal codes. That is, "right" and "duty" get their determinate and intelligible character only when the stamp of law is affixed on them. As natural rights bear no such determinate and intelligible stamp, they make *no* sense at all. Second, he finds the *Declaration* as a body of contradictory statements. He accuses the framers of this document for having their recourse to rhetorical language instead of "apt and precise expressions" to cover their "wickedness". According to him, the French *Declaration* is written,

> as if it had been an oriental tale, or an allegory for a magazine: – stale epigrams, instead of necessary distinctions, – figurative expressions preferred to simple ones – sentimental conceit as trite as they are unmeaning, preferred to apt and precise expressions – frippery ornament preferred to the majestic simplicity of good sound sense – and the acts of the senate loaded and disfigured by the tinsel of the playhouse.[7]

Like Hobbes, he feels that words be defined in precision and clarity, for the political controversy arises in the main out of verbal ambiguity and confusion. For him, the "rights of man (are) composed of a system of contradictions and

---

[7] J. Bentham, "Anarchical Fallacies" in *"Nonsense upon Stilts"*, p. 49.

impossibilities".[8] He finds lot of conceptual confusions and contradictions as lying inherent in the language of the *Declaration.* According to Bentham, rights can only be created by law, and those rights that are not created by law are contradiction in terms like "a son that never had a father", "a round square", "a species of cold heat", "a sort of dry moisture", "a kind of resplendent darkness".[9] He further asserts:

> To me a right and a legal right are the same thing, for I know no other. Right and law are correlative terms: as much so as son and father. Right is with me the child of law: from different operations of the law result different sorts of rights.[10]

Thus Bentham clarifies that there cannot be any sort of rights in abstraction from the law of the government. The natural rights that are conceived as existing outside legal framework have made them something indeterminate in character. They lack any criteria for their identification and application. That is what is called by Hart the "criterionlessness".[11] This lack of criteria for the identification of these rights gives rise to insoluble controversy in political arena. According to Bentham, their existence cannot simply be postulated as self-evident truths. That is, if we wish to have them do not mean that they exist.

> But reasons for wishing there were such things as rights, are not rights – a reason for wish that a certain right were established, is not that right – want is not supply – hunger is not bread.[12]

---

8 J. Bentham, "Anarchical Fallacies" in *"Nonsense upon Stilts"*, p. 56.

9 J. Bentham, "Supply Without Burthen or Escheat *Vice* Taxation" in *"Nonsense upon Stilts"*, pp. 72-73.

10 Ibid., p. 73.

11 H.L.A. Hart, *Essays on Bentham*, Oxford: Clarendon Press, 1982, p. 82.

12 J. Bentham, "Anarchical Fallacies" in *"Nonsense upon Stilts"*, p. 53.

Some sort of proof is needed to have their existence, which they lack.

Bentham turns to the statements of the *Declaration* to show their contradictory and absurd character. When the *Declaration* proclaims – "All men are born free", Bentham responds to this statement by calling it "absurd and miserable nonsense".[13] Men are *never* born free, he argues, but are born into subjection. He considers the case of a human child who remains dependent upon his parent in his initial years of his life, and the later years of his life, he remains bound to society. So when is he free? Bentham asks. This also holds true with the *Declaration*'s claim that "men are equal in respect of rights". If this claim is taken to be true, Bentham argues:

> The apprentice, then, is equal in rights to his master; he has as much liberty with relation to the master, as the master has with relation to him; he has as much right to command and to punish him: he is as much owner and master of the master's house, as the master himself. The case is the same as between ward and guardian. So again as between wife and husband. The madman has as good a right to confine anybody else, as anybody else has to confine him. The idiot has as much right to govern anybody, as anybody can have to govern him.[14]

This passage implies that the ideas of liberty, equality, etc. are described in the *Declaration* merely as *general* principles, without taking into consideration the natural effect their application would bring about for the people. The framers of the *Declaration* were not pragmatic enough to take into consideration whether the operation of these rights would make sense at all or would have utility in a given situation of a particular society. He concludes:

---

[13] J. Bentham, "Anarchical Fallacies" in "*Nonsense upon Stilts*", p. 50.

[14] Ibid., p. 51.

> The right itself must be *specifically* described, not jumbled with an undistinguishable heap of others, under any such vague *general* terms as property, liberty and the like.[15]

Further, a legislator's concern with social utility must recognize that he is not laying down any laws as abstract principles which are timeless and consequently applicable to all forms of society. But, unfortunately, the right to liberty, the right to equality, etc. as they have been laid down in the *Declaration* are simply abstract principles which do not have concern for specific time, place and circumstance of society. Bentham says:

> The dictates of reason and utility are the result of circumstances which require genius to discover, strength of mind to weigh and patience to investigate: the language of natural rights requires nothing but a hard front, a hard heart and an unblushing countenance. It is from the beginning to the end so much flat assertion: it neither has any thing to do with reason not will endure the mention of it.[16]

According to Bentham, every article of the *Declaration* is "hasty generalization – the great stumbling block of intellectual vanity"![17] The framers of the *Declaration* have tried to pin down the well-being of human beings in a few abstract formulations only, without regard for the continually changing circumstances of human life and society. According to Bentham, the social utility of rights arises only in the context of particular social circumstance only, and rights are to be decided accordingly. No rights, according to Bentham, can be decided once and for all circumstances as well as for all forms of society as general principles.

---

15 J. Bentham, "Anarchical Fallacies" in *"Nonsense upon Stilts"*, p. 54 (my emphasis).

16 J. Bentham, "Supply Without Burthen or Escheat *Vice* Taxation" in *"Nonsense upon Stilts"*, p. 74.

17 J. Bentham, "Anarchical Fallacies" in *"Nonsense upon Stilts"*, p. 48.

The Article II of the *Declaration* states:

> The final end of every political institution is the preservation of the natural and imprescriptible rights of man.[18]

Bentham argues against this statement by saying that there cannot be any such rights that are anterior to the government. Rather, all rights owe their existence to government.

> That there are no such things as natural rights – no such things as rights anterior to the establishment of government – no such things as natural rights opposed to, in contradistinction to, legal.[19]

As a legal positivist, Bentham attaches importance to positive law. He believes that human life in society without the rule of law would be like Hobbesian state of nature, which is a state of chaos and warfare. It is only the rule of law that can provide order and security in human life. In this context, he refers to the eighteenth-century "savage nations", where there were no governments and hence no such things as rights, security and property. So it is imperative that law should be allowed to regulate human life without, of course, undermining the happiness of the members of society. Further, it is a Utopian presumption of the proponents of the *Declaration* that government would be able to protect *all* rights of man as they argue that the sole end of the establishment of government was to guarantee the protection of these rights, which was not possible in the state of nature.[20]

---

18 "Declaration of the Rights of Man and the Citizen 1789", in *"Nonsense upon Stilts"*, p. 26.

19 J. Bentham, "Anarchical Fallacies" in *"Nonsense upon Stilts"*, p. 52.

20 Bentham deplores, like many other eighteenth-century thinkers, the idea of the origination of government by "social contract" whose end in view is supposed to be the preservation of natural rights of man. Bentham argues that "the origination of government from a →

Besides, in pointing out the mischief this nonsensical idea of rights has made to the political and social life, Bentham says that the notion of rights may incite any individual to turn out to be a rebellion of law and government. For, he may not like government's particular way of functioning on some matters of right, and may take the path of violent resistance which would create chaos, anarchy and disorder in society. Bentham even declines to talk in the language of natural rights, for that would mean, for him, using "terrorist language".[21] In social front, the rights of man threaten solidarity and cohesion in human society by encouraging its members only to pursue their selfish desires. Bentham elaborates:

> The great enemies of public peace are the selfish and dissocial passions – necessary as they are – the one to the very existence of each individual, the other to his security. On the part of these affections, a deficiency in point of strength is never to be apprehended: all that is to be apprehended in respect of them, is to be apprehended on the side of their excess. Society is held together only by the sacrifices that man can be induced to make of the gratifications they demand: to obtain these sacrifices is the great difficulty, the great task of government. What has been the object, the perpetual and palpable object, of this declaration of pretended rights? To add as much force as possible to these passions, already but too strong – to burst the cords that hold them in – to say to the selfish passions, there – everywhere – is your prey! – to the angry passions, there – everywhere – is your enemy. Such is the morality of this celebrated manifesto. . . .[22]

→ contract is a pure fiction, or in other words, a falsehood". According to him, there is no single instance of any government that has been created by social contract. Rather, all governments are formed by force and established gradually by habit. See "Anarchical Fallacies", *"Nonsense upon Stilts"*, p. 55.

21 J. Bentham, "Anarchical Fallacies", in *"Nonsense upon Stilts"*, p. 53.

22 Ibid., p. 48.

As a hedonist, Bentham identifies the self-interest as the core of human nature, and he does not deny its intrinsic necessity for human survival and security. But the exclusive pursuit of self-interest, Bentham believes, would result in chaos and disorder in social relationships. But unfortunately the doctrine of natural rights, as it is based on individualism, indulges the immediate and unconditional gratification of individual desires, and thereby it would weaken the social bond that exists among its members. As an altruist, Bentham visualizes the possibility of human society as depending on individual's pursuit of those interests that are not exclusively his own.

Edmund Burke: Natural Rights as "Pretended Rights"

Burke deplores the legitimacy of the French Revolution and vehemently criticizes the subsequently adopted French *Declaration* which is based on the Lockean conception of natural rights. According to Burke, drawing any parallelism between the English Glorious Revolution of 1688 and the French Revolution of 1789 is quite misleading. For, the English Revolution of 1688 was an acceptable and desirable change within the English Constitutional framework, and it had no intention of overthrowing all past laws and liberties. Burke had high regard for the existing social tradition and its indisputable laws and conventions. He believes in incremental change in social and political life and not in perfect *status quo*. He disapproved the sudden and abrupt change in social and political order as it happened to be the case at the time of French Revolution. According to him, the French Revolution was a misguided attempt to overthrow all past laws and conventions of the *ancien regime* and to establish a new social and political order based on the principles, such as the abstract rationalism, the rights of man and popular sovereignty. Burke deplored the French revolutionaries' attempt to create an altogether new social and political order on the basis of their leading ideas – including the universal rights of man along with democratic principles that stem from these ideas.

It is to be noted at the outset that Burke does not oppose the idea of rights *per se* as he intends to defend "the real rights of man" against "the pretended rights"[23] of the natural rights theorists. That is to say, he pleads for inherited, customary or what he calls "prescriptive" rights of man. In fact, Burke as an active member of the British Parliament was all along critical of the British rule in India which had been consciously violating the traditional laws, rights and customs of its Indian subjects.

Though he agrees with Locke that political philosophy has to be based on theological foundation, he rejects the idea of deriving the equality of man from the premise that human beings are created equal by the Almighty. He also rejects substantially the idea of rights of man as it is understood in the natural rights tradition. J. Waldron rightly points out:

> Though he was not averse to the rhetorical deployment of the language of rights and even, on occasion, the language of the social contract, Burke appears to have rejected the substance of many of the ideas that, for us at least, mark out the natural rights movement as an interesting and distinct philosophical and political tradition. Thus, for instance, he rejected the idea that the mere fact of our humanity endowed us with rights which were of serious significance for the evaluation of current political arrangements; in fact he rejected the whole approach which based our present rights on considerations in principle independent of the evolved political and social system of the society in which we live.[24]

---

23 E. Burke, *Reflections on the Revolution in France*, London: Everyman's Library, 1967, p. 56.

24 J. Waldron, "Introduction", Burke's *Reflections on the Revolution in France*, in *"Nonsense upon Stilts"*, p. 83.

Burke refutes the arguments of natural rights theorists mainly on the following three grounds. First, for Burke, the idea of the rights of man is an abstract conception of rights and hence meaningless and simplistic. The conception of natural rights that is promulgated in the French *Declaration* is conceived as a derivative of the law of nature by its innovator John Locke and others. The law of nature is a metaphysical principle that is supposed to regulate the life of man in the "state of nature" prior to the appearance of civil society. These rights that are supposed to have been enjoyed by individuals as inhabitants of the state of nature are not "real" rights but "imagined" ones. These apparently revolutionary ideas are not derived from the realization of the complexities of existing societies, and hence they have not evolved through shared social and political experience. That is to say, the idea of the rights of man has not evolved out of concrete historical experiences. Burke further argues that the theory of natural rights is untested, that is to say, they have not been applied to any concrete social and political situation. So the prediction of the natural rights exponents that the promulgation of them would bring about the creation of a new social and political order is bound to fail. They are nothing but "metaphysical abstraction".

Second, according to Burke, the social and political changes have their own course, and such changes take place only gradually, and *no* abstract idea such as the rights of man is capable of bringing about new social and political order all on a sudden. The talk of universal natural rights in abstraction from particular communities makes no sense at all. The idea of natural rights, according to Burke, is simplistic in nature. For, they are not the outcome of complex social and political experiences; nor they take into account the web of complex relationships among the members of certain community. Burke writes:

> But I cannot stand forward, and give praise or blame to any thing which relates to human actions, and human concerns, on a simple view of the object, as it stands stripped of every relation, in all the nakedness and solitude of metaphysical abstraction. Circumstances (which with some gentlemen pass for nothing) give in reality to every political principle its distinguishing colour, and discriminating effect. The circumstances are what render every civil and political scheme beneficial or noxious to mankind.[25]

For Burke, rights are social in origin and foundation. That is, there cannot be any right in abstraction from particular societies as it has been conceived of by natural rights thinkers. Social and political circumstances determine the distinctive character of rights. For, human beings are social creatures bound by some relationships and communal obligations. But the doctrine of the "rights of man" does not take into account what Waldron calls "circumstantial evaluation".[26] It is simply a "metaphysical abstraction" which does not take into account all the "infinite modifications" of time and circumstance that determine the practical feasibility of a proposal. Further, the natural rights theorists ignore the fact that there *are* differences among societies in terms of its history, geography, climate and tradition, which determine the distinctive character of these societies' particular legal and political arrangements, and hence rights. The proponents of the French *Declaration*, Burke argues, have erred in claiming the universality of rights ignoring the national differences that would have their effect in the application of the content of the *Declaration*. There cannot be any political proposal like the rights of man that is valid for all times and places. For Burke, there is nothing in politics that can be stated in axioms and would be valid irrespective of place and time. According to burke,

---

25 E. Burke, *Reflections on the Revolution in France*, p. 6.

26 J. Waldron, "Introduction", Burke's *Reflections on the Revolution in France*, in *"Nonsense upon Stilts"*, p. 85.

> Political reason is a computing principle; adding, subtracting, multiplying, and dividing, morally and not metaphysically or mathematically, true moral denominations.[27]

Third, the doctrine of natural rights is dangerous from political perspective as it threatens to destroy all inherited and established institutions, laws and "prescriptive" rights. The conception of natural rights is "metaphysically true", but "morally and politically false".[28] As the rights of man are untested political proposal, their application might have practical effect of subverting those rights that are actually in practice in societies. Burke had profound respect for existent social tradition and argues against imposing alien ways of life on existing folkways based on the conception of natural rights. For, any attempt to implement these abstract rights may go against inherited and customary rights and ultimately bring about their total annihilation, which are actual foundations of human society. Further, the conception of universal rights of man provides a theoretical perspective from which an individual can critically evaluate the existing laws and institutions. If it is found that the existing laws and institutions do not meet the standard, that is, of the rights of man, then individuals may turn out to be violent protesters, and thereby they may create chaos and disorder in the society.

The point that needs stressing here is that Burke does not reject the rights altogether but only calls into question the *basis* of the radical doctrine of the French revolutionaries. He actually defends the "real" rights that are recognized by the existing social and political institutions, which play an important role to satisfy human wants and needs. These rights are an "entailed inheritance" in the sense that they have been handed down from one generation to another.

---

27 E. Burke, *Reflections on the Revolution in France*, pp. 59-60.

28 Ibid., p. 59.

While Burke rejects "the rights of men", he admits and defends what he calls "the *real* rights of men". Fennessy argues that Burke has made a distinction between rights as individual privileges and rights as relation.[29] If we imagine that there are separate and discrete individuals living in a hypothetical state of nature, then we can bestow each of them certain advantages, privileges and prerogatives. These are given to each of them in the form of food, shelter, medical facilities, etc. for their survival. These privileges become *rights* when we give them moral approval. Burke has never denied their necessity in human life and the validity of giving them the moral sanction. What is his objection against these rights-privileges is that they are pure abstractions based on a hypothesis or a condition outside society, or "prior to" society. In such a condition "by having a right to everything they want everything".[30] What the natural rights thinkers call "rights" are nothing but needs by another name; these are for Burke not real rights. In civil society and under government such unlimited needs in the name of rights no longer hold, simply because the hypothesis of unsocial condition under which men are attributed the so-called rights has lost its relevance. According to Burke, "man cannot enjoy the rights of an uncivil and of a civil state together".[31]

In contrast, what Burke calls "the *real* rights of men" are not needs of separate individuals but something that arise out of the relation between men in civil society. In civil society, men are bound together by moral relationships which give rise to moral obligations. This relation is, in the main, meant for making provision for human wants. Human wants are

---

[29] R.R. Fennessy, *Burke, Paine and the Rights of Man: A Difference of Political Opinion*, The Hague: Martinus Nijhoff, 1963, p. 139.

[30] E. Burke, *Reflections on the Revolution in France*, p. 57.

[31] Ibid.

fulfilled by goods and legitimate institutions of civil society and government. Whatever is his advantage becomes his right in civil society where men live in moral relationship with one another. Such rights are for Burke are "entailed inheritance". While referring to inherited rights and liberties of Englishmen, Burke writes:

> You will observe, that from Magna Carta to the Declaration of Right, it has been the uniform policy of our constitution to claim and assert our liberties, as an *entailed inheritance* derived to us from our forefathers, and to be transmitted to our posterity; as an estate specially belonging to the people of this kingdom, without any reference whatever to any other more general or prior right.[32]

Burke accuses the French revolutionaries for their excessive faith in reason in understanding society and politics. He deplores the political theorists of his time, including the exponents of the doctrine of natural rights, for their obsession with a priori deductive reasoning and applying it beyond arithmetical operation. According to Burke, the faculty of reason is capable of providing intellectuals with clear and distinct ideas which stand in precise and ordered in relation to one another, and *this* is true with regard to arithmetical operation. But in politics, such precision and order have little value. Like arithmetic, there is nothing clear and distinct in social and political affairs. Burke points out that reason has its limits to make it the basis of authority, rights and law, that is of social and political life. The apriorism of the *Declaration* of rights is nothing but mere abstraction.

In conclusion, we may note that Burke's criticism of the natural rights seems to have some similarities with that of Bentham. Like Bentham, Burke denies rationalistic approach to politics. He recognizes the importance of circumstances

[32] E. Burke, *Reflections on the Revolution in France*, p. 31.

which render all civil and political proposals like the rights of man, beneficial or harmful to human beings. Any social and political scheme would have value only when they are effective in bringing about happiness to mankind. Further, like Bentham, he also finds the talk of rights to be meaningless in abstraction from particular circumstances of actual and existing communities. Moreover, one also finds some utilitarian strands in Burke, as it is evident from the following statement:

> What is the use of discussing a man's abstract right to food or medicine? The question is upon the method of procuring and administering them. In that deliberation I shall always advise to call in the aid of the farmer and the physician, rather than professor of metaphysics.[33]

But one cannot proceed further, as there are obvious differences between them:

1. Burke's conception of human well-being is not based on hedonism as it is the case with Bentham.
2. Burke's view does not fall under any formal theory like Bentham's utilitarianism.
3. Burke argues for maximization of the happiness of people on the basis of morality and not on the basis of formal and articulate calculation as Bentham proposes.

Karl Marx: Natural Rights as Rights of "Egoistic" Man

Marx was quite aware of the fact that the modern conception of natural or human rights is a part of liberal democratic tradition which has founded it on the belief in what is called "the law of nature". The latter is conceived to be a metaphysical principle according to which the order of nature is capable of providing us with the standard of what we ought to do. That

[33] E. Burke, *Reflections on the Revolution in France*, p. 58.

is, the natural world order exhibits an eternal and immutable moral characteristic which men have to conform with. But Marx right away rejects the belief in an eternal moral order along with all claims of natural law theory. According to him, the conception of natural right as derivative of the natural law, which is formulated by Enlightenment thinkers, are fundamental to bourgeois society. The conception of the law of nature and the natural rights, Marx argues, is a part of idealistic imagination and no evidence can be adduced in support of them. And consequently, the rights of man are designed as part of bourgeois ideology to serve the interest of the ruling class of bourgeois state.

Marx criticizes individualism as it revolves around the modern theories of rights. In his analysis of individualism in the capitalist society, two conflicting views of man are accommodated. On the one hand, man is regarded as an abstract, self-determining and free individual. On the other, man is viewed as a saleable commodity, alienable object and a slave of the capitalist society. Let us analyse these two views taking one at a time. An individual is entitled to enjoy rights not due to any status or relationship which he may occupy in society. That is, the right in a capitalist society is conferred on an individual for not being a doctor, teacher, mother, lord, etc. These rights are conferred on him independently of all such relationships or circumstances. In this context, an individual is taken to be an *abstract* individual rather than a *concrete* individual. In this abstract sense, an individual is considered to be self-determining and free individual. That is, he is free to decide which capitalist he will work for and thereby alienate his labour power. Individual as right holder in this abstract sense are *discrete* individuals always busy pursuing his own private interests and aspirations. This individualistic form of rights implies a society in which the interest of each individual stands in opposition to the interest of the other. Each person is an egoist in such a society. Thus at a preliminary stage, the liberty to pursue one's own interests and aspirations is limited by the interests of others. But gradually with growing tendency of egoistic pursuit of self-interests, society is reduced to a war zone of private interests and aspirations. In such a situation, the state steps in and imposes certain restrictions and bindings upon the conduct of selfish individuals in order to forge a unity among them and thereby keeps the society in integration. But this unity, for Marx, is a false unity having no strong *social* foundation but only an artificial basis provided by the law. On the other hand, Marx draws another picture of individual living in a capitalist society. Here, he is viewed as "profane" object that is saleable as a commodity. Just as the capitalist purchases various raw materials which go into the production of a commodity, so too he purchases another special commodity which the worker provides by their skills, services and powers. This is the worker's labour-power which is the sole source of surplus value, and it is the latter which goes into making profit for the capitalist.

Marx talks of (i) human rights, (ii) the rights of man, and (iii) the rights of the citizen. The term "human rights" is the general name for other two kinds of rights. He distinguishes between the rights of man and the rights of the citizen. The latter kind of rights is the rights of political participation, such as the right to vote, and the former includes: (1) the right to freedom of expression, (2) the right to liberty, (3) the right to equality, (4) the right to property, and (5) the right to security. Marx begins his critique of each of these rights with a general remark which provides the direction of his arguments. He writes:

> Above all we notice the fact that the so-called rights of man, the rights of man as different from the rights of the citizen are nothing but the rights of the member of civil society, i.e.

> egoistic man, man separated from other man and the community.[34]

The expression "civil society" in the passage refers to the capitalist society where the means of production is owned by private organizations, where there is a market for all kinds of commodities, including labour-power, and where there is rampant growth of industries. In such a society, the egoistic and selfish individuals with no relation with other man and group enjoy the so-called rights of man. Marx's criticism of these rights is as follows.

THE RIGHT TO FREEDOM OF EXPRESSION

As regards the right to religious freedom or the freedom of conscience, Marx points out that the religion no longer plays any role in the life of a state. Even though it is no longer treated as the spirit of the state, it is treated of course as the spirit of civil society. In the latter, it becomes a private right expressing crude egoism. For Marx,

> It (religion) has become the expression of separation of man from his common essence, from himself and from other men, as it was originally. It is still only the abstract recognition of a particular perversion, private whim, and arbitrariness. . . . It is shoved away into the crowd of private interests and exiled from the common essence as such.[35]

THE RIGHT TO LIBERTY

The right to liberty in the capitalist society does not mean unbridled freedom but the freedom limited by others. The freedom of the individual has its fenced-off domain where others have *no* entrance.[36] Each discrete and isolated individual

---

34 K. Marx "On the Jewish Question" in *"Nonsense upon Stilts"*, p. 145.

35 Ibid., p. 142.

36 As Leszek Kolakowski clarifies, "For to the Marxist, both the concept of liberty and the idea of human rights, as defined by Enlightenment →

enjoys his freedom within certain limits, by being confined himself in a fully fortified world set by law. While scrutinizing the French revolutionary Declaration and Constitution, Marx writes:

> Thus freedom is the right to do and perform what does not harm others. The limits within which each person can move without harming others is defined by the law, just as the boundary between two fields is defined by the fence. The freedom in question is that of a man treated as an isolated monad and withdrawn into himself. . . . But the right of man to freedom is not based on the union of man with man, but on the separation of man from man. It is the right to this separation, the rights of the limited individual who is limited to himself.[37]

Thus, according to Marx, individual in the capitalist society is invested with rights not as concrete and socially situated human being, but as an *abstract* individual who is taken out of the context of society and apart from all relationships.

THE RIGHT TO EQUALITY

Apart from the right to liberty that is discussed above, there is the right to equality which, in the bourgeois society, means the equality of *abstract* individuals and not the equality of concrete human beings living in society. In a concrete and

---

→ thinkers and ideologists of the French Revolution, are the specific expressions of a bourgeois society that is on the verge of collapse. Marx's writings, from the 'Jewish question' onward, are wholly dismissive of all claims made to the lasting validity of 'bourgeois freedom' and unremovable human rights. The idea of the individual's rights, Marx explains, implies a society in which the interests of each person is naturally and inevitably opposed to the interests of others, a society incurably torn asunder by the clash of private aspirations." See his "Marxism and Human Rights", *Daedalus*, Journal of the American Academy of Arts and Sciences, **112** no. 4, Fall 1983.

37 K. Marx, "On the Jewish Question", in *"Nonsense upon Stilts"*, p. 146.

social situation, man finds himself as belonging to different classes where equality of men is nothing but an illusion. For, man in the bourgeois society possesses unequal property and resources, and hence they are unequal in respect of capacities and the opportunities they get. The majority of individuals, who are workers and labourers, belong to the class of proletariat, and they are incessantly exploited by those a few people called "the capitalists" who control the mode of production. Though the worker enjoys considerable freedom in choosing whom he will work for, he ultimately remains as a slave of the capitalist class. So the unequal status of individuals remains to be an inevitable fact in a bourgeois society. Thus the right to equality though applicable to all, the application of the equality is only formal, and hence the rights the individual *enjoys* are not equal. Here, the equality of individual means merely a *formal* equality. The equality as a counterpart of liberty is simply that each man is treated without discrimination as a "self-sufficient monad". In a bourgeois society, the right to equality as a *formal* right gets recognition in its legal framework and thus given institutional recognition. But its application varies in accordance with the class-status of the individual. "Thus in the capitalist society, men have formally equal but substantively unequal right."[38]

THE RIGHT TO PRIVATE PROPERTY

In his consideration of the right to private property, Marx points out that the owner of the property is entitled to enjoy it or to dispose of it at his will without regard for others. Owning property by an individual makes him an isolated egoist deriving his enjoyment from the property, and

---

[38] B. Parekh, "The Modern Conception of Right and Its Marxist Critique" in Upendra Baxi (ed.) *The Right to Be Human*, New Delhi: Lancer International in association with India International Centre, 1987, p. 18.

wherefrom his fellow-men are excluded. For, no other individual is allowed to share the enjoyment of property, and thus property becomes simply a means of fulfilling some selfish desire of the individual. Hence the freedom of the individual is limited by the freedom of others. Marx puts:

> Thus the right of man to property is the right to enjoy his possessions and dispose of the same arbitrarily, without regard for other men, independently from society, the right of selfishness. It is the former individual freedom together with its latter application that forms the basis of civil society. It leads man to see in other men not the realization but the limitation of his own freedom.[39]

THE RIGHT TO SECURITY

The right to security consists in ensuring each of the members of a civil society the protection of his person, liberty and property. It is considered to be the highest social concept in the civil society. But, according to Marx, the concept of security is nothing but "the assurance of egoism".[40] For, the right to security is meant for providing an individual with guarantee to enjoy *all* of his rights – the right to life, liberty and property. The various rights that are discussed above, according to Marx, are based on selfish and private gains, and their application disintegrates the social bond that exists among human beings.

But, for Marx, "man is a species-being".[41] In his thought, man is no longer a discrete and an isolated individual but is possessed of all the same species-character. It is only human individuals, and not animals, who are bound by species-relationships. An individual stands united with his fellow-men because of this species-character. This species-character of man

---

[39] K. Marx, "On the Jewish Question" in *"Nonsense upon Stilts"*, p. 146.

[40] K. Marx, "On the Jewish Question" in *"Nonsense upon Stilts"*, p. 147.

[41] K. Marx, *Economic and Philosophic Manuscripts of 1844*, Moscow: Progress Publishers, 5th edn., 1977, p. 72.

finds expression in his social and communal life. According to Marx, it is the modern theory of rights that alienates man from his fellow-men and disintegrates the unity of the human species. Rather than being appreciative of his social nature and of his essential dependence on others, the bourgeois society turns each individual into an "isolated monad, withdrawn into himself". By denying the social nature of man and his essential dependence on others for survival and emancipation, the rights of man tear asunder the species-bond of man and replace it with the egoism and selfish need of man.[42] It is because of this egoistic pursuit of interests and aspirations in the bourgeois society that the relations among the members of civil society can never be smooth and friendly relations. Rather, each individual develops a hostile attitude towards the other. Marx concludes:

> Thus none of the so-called rights of man goes beyond egoistic man, man as he is in civil society, namely an individual withdrawn behind his private interests and whims, and separated from the community. Far from the rights of man conceiving of man as a species-being, species-life itself, society, appears as a framework exterior to individuals, a limitation of their original self-sufficiency. The only bond that holds them together is natural necessity, need and private interest, the conservation of their property and egoistic person.[43]

---

42 As G.G. Brenkert clarifies, "The notion of rights which might hold simply because one was a human individual, independently of the society in which one lived, had no basis. What we see culminating in capitalism is the development, through various historical measures, of individuals who are identifiable without reference to their positions, roles, or relations to others, but are identifiable simply as human beings qua possessors or owners of labor power." See his "Marx and Human Rights", *Journal of the History of Philosophy*, XXIV no. I, January 1986.

43 K. Marx, "On the Jewish Question", in *"Nonsense upon Stilts"*, p. 147.

From a careful study of Marx's thought, it seems that he does not reject human rights altogether. What he sees as his task is to cleanse it of bourgeois perversions. He rejects the bourgeois foundation of human rights on abstract individual. That is, human rights cannot be based on man as rational being who is capable of choice but on the *effective* role he plays in society. He sees human emancipation in the transformation of man's material condition by participating in the productive economic life and not in his abstract nature. Marx anticipates human emancipation in his participation in the productive life of society and thereby ushering in a communist era. Until and unless the stage of communist socialism is reached, according to Marx, the rights of man in some form or other may be retained as a matter of tactics but not as a matter of principles. But with the beginning of conflictless and unified communist era, the so-called rights of man lose their relevance. It is only man's participation in the productive life of society as a component of the collective "whole", rather than as an isolated individual, that paves the way for his emancipation.

Some Other Critical Reactions

In the present section, we would deal with the critique of natural rights put forward by two contemporary thinkers – D.G. Ritchie and Margaret MacDonald – taking one at a time.

D.G. RITCHIE

His book *Natural Rights* opens up with a historical review of various conceptions of natural law and natural rights that have dominated the political and ethical theories from the Greeks down to the eighteenth century. In the fifth chapter, he turns to the criticism of the traditional conception of natural law and natural rights, and presents his own view on rights. To begin with, Ritchie has recourse to quotations from others' writings to define what a right is in both legal and moral senses. By legal rights, he understands a capacity of an individual to influence and control the actions of others with the approval and assistance of the state. The legal right is a kind of claim made by a person to restrain others' actions, and this is approved by the law of the land. The law of a state stands behind and entitles him to make such a claim upon other citizens. In the similar fashion, a moral right is meant to be a capacity of a person to impose restraint upon others' conduct with concurrence and assistance of, at least having no opposition from, public opinion. The claim of a right in moral sense is in need of approval and backing from private individuals only, regardless of state's recognition. The point here is that there may well be disputes and disagreements with regard to both legal and moral rights. But while there are courts to make appeal to resolve the disputes and disagreements in case of legal rights, there is no such courts for moral rights where appeal can be made to have an abiding decision. It is due to the imprecise nature of moral rights that it becomes difficult to determine with regard to what cases and to what extent a person can enjoy moral rights. Besides, the prevalent public opinions change and differ with regard to moral matters, and this makes the situation further complicated.

According to Ritchie, it is in order to obviate these difficulties, the moral and political philosophers presume the law of nature and natural rights to be the ideal standard with reference to which all moral and political rights could be deduced. Says Ritchie:

> Natural rights are not identical with moral rights, because in many cases people have claimed that they had a natural right to do things that were not recognized either by the law of the land or by the prevalent public opinion or by the conscience of the *average* individual. Natural rights, when alleged by the would-be reformer, mean those rights which in his opinion would be recognized by the public opinion

> of such a society as he admires, and would either be supported or at least would not be interfered with by its laws, if it had any laws; they are the rights which he thinks ought to be recognized, i.e. they are the rights sanctioned by his ideal society, whatever that may be.[44]

The fundamental question he raises now is: What determines rights? He right away rejects the external authority of any form as basis of natural or fundamental rights, and in this context, he criticizes Hobbes. Appealing to Nature too, according to Ritchie, cannot provide us with an ideal standard on which rights can be founded. Like Bentham, Ritchie rejects the law of nature as the court of appeal to settle the issue of the rights of man. But he refuses to ground the rights of man on the greatest happiness principle following Bentham. The difficulty that arises for him with regard to the law of nature is that of interpreting the "voice" of Nature. For the law of Nature admits of no analysis by rational means. To make an appeal to the law of nature means rejecting all attempts to argue from experience. Thus Ritchie rejects the law of nature and brings in the idea of "utility" to articulate a possible ground for the consideration of rights.

MARGARET MACDONALD

She begins her critique of natural rights by raising the following questions: What is the nature of propositions concerning natural rights? How do the confusions about them arise? MacDonald writes:

> Propositions about natural law and natural rights are not generalizations from experience or deductions from observed facts subsequently confirmed by experience.[45]

---

44 D.G. Ritchie, *Natural Rights*, London: George Allen & Unwin, 1924, p. 80.

45 M. MacDonald, "Natural Rights", in Jeremy Waldron (ed.) *Theories of Rights*, Oxford: Oxford University Press, 1984, p. 25.

Then how are they discovered? According to MacDonald's account of the natural rights doctrine, they are known not as totally disconnected from natural fact, but "as entailed by the intrinsic or essential nature of man".[46] The natural fact of man is that he possesses reason or rationality which is intrinsic to him, and it is reason which enables him to know the natural law. Human reason determines what ought to be, i.e. the ideal standard. Man's reason enables him to deduce the ideal from the natural fact, i.e. from the fact that man is rational. It is the fact of being rational that makes him similar to his fellow-beings and different from all beasts.

MacDonald argues that though the possession of reason is a natural characteristic of man, which makes him similar to his fellow-beings and different from brutes, yet it is simply a natural or empirical fact about man among many of his characteristics, and this cannot be the reason to elevate the natural characteristic into an essence or to consider it as intrinsic property of man. The natural rights thinkers are wrong in their supposition that man possesses a fixed or finished nature, and that he is destined to pursue some definite ends in fulfilment of such a nature. According to MacDonald, the fact of being rational cannot set the standard of value. In fact, man has no essential or intrinsic property at all that entails what ought to be. Man is not definable at all as he does not possess any such *defining* characteristic like reason. Reason is only one empirical characteristic of man among his multiple characteristics, and this, being an empirical fact, cannot set the standard of what ought to be.

Further, MacDonald puts forward another objection against natural rights theorists who hold that it is reason as man's essential characteristic that enables him to *know* the propositions about natural law and natural rights. In her

---

46 M. MacDonald, "Natural Rights", in *Theories of Rights*, p. 25.

words, "The standard of natural law is set by reason and is known because men have reason".[47] But propositions that are known by reason are classified by MacDonald as tautologies or analytical propositions which state rules for the uses of symbols or which follow from such rules within a linguistic and logical system. According to her account of traditional doctrine, "men have natural rights" means a barren tautology, namely, "x is human entails x has natural rights".[48] These propositions are distinctive of being neither the statement of facts nor the assertion of value. What reason can know are only the analytic propositions or tautologies. Hence man's ability to reason does not entail propositions of natural law and natural rights. MacDonald concludes:

> Because it is confused on these distinctions, the theory of natural law and natural rights constantly confounds reason with right and both with matter of fact and existence. The fact that men do reason is thought to be somehow a natural or empirical confirmation of what is logically deduced by reason as a standard by which to judge the imperfections of what exists.[49]

MacDonald now turns to consider the notion of reason and its relation to man's right-claims. She points out that man is by definition a rational animal, and this is so considered since the time of Aristotle. The exponents of natural rights theories belong to this tradition. To be rational means various mental activities including the capacity to think abstractly. It is this characteristic of being rational, which is peculiar to human beings and differentiates them from brutes. It is again this feature that has been taken by the advocates of natural law to be the defining characteristic of man. They have made it the

---

47 M. MacDonald, "Natural Rights", in *Theories of Rights*, p. 25.

48 Ibid., p. 27.

49 Ibid., p. 26.

basis of equality of men and natural rights. But MacDonald argues that human beings share many other activities, such as hunting, fighting and adapting suitable means to end with other animals, which seldom need abstract thinking. Even in their activities of higher order such as participating in artistic activities, we rarely find the trace of abstraction. So there is no role of any "constant factor" like reason or rationality in these human activities. MacDonald agrees that the claim of rights is not made by savages, oppressed or downtrodden but by such people who have reached a certain level of their intellectual development. Marx and Engels, she cites as example, were not themselves wage-labourers, but they claimed rights and fought for on behalf of industrial labourers. But MacDonald does not deny the role of reason in her account of natural rights but reduces it to a minimum. She says:

> It is generally agreed that the doctrines of natural rights, natural law, and the social contract, are individualistic. To claim rights as an individual independently of society, a man must have reached a level of self-consciousness which enables him to isolate himself in thought from his social environment. This presupposes a considerable capacity for abstraction. To this extent natural rights, or the ability to claim natural rights, depends on reason. But it does not follow from this that reason alone constitutes the specific nature of man or that the worth of human beings is determined solely by their IQs. Reason is only one human excellence.[50]

Thus in opposition to the exponents of natural rights, MacDonald denies reason being the essence of man that constitutes his specific nature. She even denies having any uniform and common nature shared by all members of human species. There can be no fixed and immutable nature same in

---

[50] M. MacDonald, "Natural Rights", in *Theories of Rights*, p. 29.

all human beings. Nor are they somehow bound to pursue certain common ends set for the human race to fulfil his fixed nature.[51] In opposition to M. Maritain who argues for fixed human nature and common ends corresponding to his natural constitution, she argues that human beings are not created to fulfil the common ends of human species just as piano is built to produce certain attuned sounds.

Conclusion

We may note here the main points of criticism against the doctrine of natural rights, which have been elaborated above. First, Bentham provides both philosophical and political arguments against the conception of natural rights, which have found place in the French "Declaration of the Rights of Man and the Citizen" of 1789. He rejects the French *Declaration* as a body of meaningless statements – "nonsense upon stilts". As a legal positivist, he believes in rights that are a part of legal procedure. Since the idea of natural rights does not have legal status it has no existence at all. Politically, he finds the talks of rights as one of the possible causes of incitement among individuals who may turn out to be rebels of law and government, and thereby creating chaos and disharmony in the state.

Second, Burke argues that the natural rights are abstract in nature and hence they are not "real" rights. For him, the

---

[51] For MacDonald, since men have no fixed nature, they cannot have any defining characteristic, and hence they cannot be defined. That is, the concept of man is an open-textured concept and hence it admits of no definition. According to MacDonald, "Human beings are not like exactly similar bottles of whisky each marked 'for export only' or some device indicating a common destination or end. Men do not share a fixed nature, nor, therefore, are there any ends which they must necessarily pursue in fulfilment of such nature. There is no definition of 'man.'" See her "Natural Rights", in *Theories of Rights*, pp. 29-30.

"real" rights evolve out of social relations. Besides, the rights of man are an untested political proposal, in the sense that the application of them in society would disrupt those rights that are actually in practice in society.

Third, Ritchie argues that the law of nature, from which the idea of natural rights is said to have derived, admits of no rational analysis, and hence it cannot be the ideal standard upon which the notion of rights can be founded.

Last, according to natural rights theorists, the law of nature and the natural rights are standards by which the existing human conditions are judged, and these standards are known by reason, which is regarded as intrinsic property of man. But MacDonald argues that the characteristic of being rational is simply an empirical fact, which does not constitute man's specific nature, and hence it cannot set the standard of what ought to be.

5

The Western World-view and Natural Rights

An Assessment

THE idea of natural rights, which has been elaborated along with its critiques in the last two chapters, is philosophically based on some principles which constitute the part of the Western world-view. In order to delve deeper into the philosophical dimension of the natural rights paradigm it is worthwhile to identify and analyse the various characteristics of the Western world-view that have affected its formulation. There are several characteristics of the Western world-view, such as individualism, rationality, patriarchy, colonialism, racism and progress. In the first place, the Western modernism focuses on man as an individual rather than as a social being. The Enlightenment thinkers, such as Voltaire, Locke, Adam Smith and others were concerned with individual freedom and progress. They also wanted to liberate the individual from all kinds of superstitions by laying stress on scientific knowledge. Further, they emphasized the rationality and logical thinking of man. For them, reason is the only mode of human knowledge. Furthermore, the Western world-view was also characteristically patriarchal in character. Women's history and achievements have almost been excluded from the historical record, although the feminist movement has, to some extent, compensated this lacuna in recent times. Moreover, the West has a long history of colonialism and racism as part of its world-view. The notion of progress is also ingrained in the Western world-view, which requires that human beings are always in need of moving towards their growth and development. In what follows, we shall confine ourselves only to two prominent features of the Western world-view, which have played a major role in formulating the natural rights theories – individualism and rationality.

The Primacy of the Individual

The Western world-view focuses on human individual and his nature. All values, concepts and practices including rights of this world-view revolve round the conception of the individual. It is the needs and interests of the individual that are at the centre of the Western world-view. In the feudal period of Europe, there has been little importance of the needs and interests of the individual possessing personal and unique identity. Peoples' identities and choices were determined by the identities and choices of their family, social group, or community. That human individual has his uniqueness and choice of his own in terms of his needs and interests have seldom been heeded. It is only after the feudalism collapsed that people became able to think of themselves as not necessarily a part of his social class or group but as *individuals.* The new intellectual climate, which is known variously as the Enlightenment or the Age of Reason, allowed the rational and scientific explanation of society in *personal* terms.

The dominant ideology that propagates the conception of rights in the Western tradition is known as liberalism. As the principal ideology of the modernist culture it focuses on the individual and his rights. If we see from a broader perspective, we would realize that individual's social and political experience is given supreme importance and value in the Western world-view. The individual achievements get distinction and honour, and finally celebrated. The historical events that took place manifestly in collective efforts are highlighted as the achievement of the individuals. Columbus's discovery of America is considered as the individual achievement without giving credit to the sailors who sailed the ship. Napoleon's defeat at the hands of Wellington at Waterloo is highlighted as the achievement of Wellington alone without any role of the soldiers who actually fought. Hitler is blamed for evil event like the Second World War without taking into account any social, political and historical contribution that had led to the disaster.[1] Thus human achievement is broadly looked upon as an individual success story, while the blame is also put again on the *individual* human being for any evil event or disaster.

While denouncing, on the one hand, all forms of absolute and arbitrary power, and religious conformity, the liberal tradition of the West emphasizes the moral belief in equal and intrinsic moral worth of the individual on the other. Human beings in the Western world-view came to be regarded basically as *individuals*. They are viewed from moral perspective as *prior* to society or community. Each person is regarded to be of special value. This distinctive stress on the individuality of human person encouraged to think of each individual as possessing a set of inherent rights. Individuals are the bearers of natural rights by virtue of being human only. In what is called the natural rights tradition, individuals are conceived to have existence temporally *prior* to the appearance of any society. So their rights are taken to be prior to the social institutions, and the good of the individual is taken to be morally prior to the collective good. The primacy of the individual over society leads to the view that the latter is nothing but the collection of individuals who are always busy pursuing their own personal needs and interests. On

---

1 These examples are taken from Jim Ife's *Human Rights and Social Work*, Cambridge: Cambridge University Press, 2001, pp. 60-61.

this view, an individual is egoistic and largely self-sufficient in nature and owes nothing to society for his flourishing and growth. The excessive stress on the needs and interests of the individual leads to the thinking of society as almost non-existent. Let us turn to the specific thinkers, such as Hobbes, Locke and Paine who stick to the principle of individualism in their theories of rights.

THOMAS HOBBES

Chronologically, it is Hobbes who has made first ever attempt to bring into focus man as an *individual* who is hitherto lost in society. The chapter entitled "On Man" in the *Leviathan,* he recognizes the importance of the individual, and describes the psychology of individual, irrespective of his social class or status. Here, his object of analysis is man as *discrete* individual, considered apart from all relationships with any association or community.

If individualism is taken to be the one side of a coin, then the political absolutism is the other side of the same coin in Hobbes' political philosophy, and one cannot be understood without the other. He agrees to grant absolute power to any political regime only if the peace and the security of the person and his property are guaranteed by it. The foundation of the state or society is laid by free and equal individuals who are egoistic and selfish in nature on the basis of their mutual consent. The element of consent provides the legitimacy to the sovereign to regulate human affairs. The all-powerful sovereign can perpetuate its rule for an indefinite period so long as it does not threaten the life of the individual. On Hobbes' view, society or state is a co-operative enterprise which would lose its rationale for existence if it no longer comes to the benefit and well-being of the individuals. For, it is the individuals to whom the all-powerful sovereign state owes its existence. Hobbes allows individuals the rights to resist the sovereign state if the latter threatens individual's self-preservation which is absolute "right of nature". Although the Hobbesian individual is the building-block of the edifice of the sovereign state, he does not disappear into the latter. Hobbes grants the individual the right to have private space, i.e. his thoughts, feelings and economics which are kept beyond the reach of the sovereign state.

The Hobbesian man is completely ego-centric, isolated and solitary individual who is always in motion to satisfy his desires and appetites. He has his own unique sensual reaction to the physical world around him, and his behaviour pattern does not conform to any moral rule. The pursuit of desires and passions by each individual, without regard for others, gives rise to conflict of interests among men. He remains under constant fear of attack, and hence remains alert to self-defence. Thus Hobbes' system is dominated by individual psychology of fear and self-defence.

Despite being an apostle of absolutism, Hobbes' sovereign state is only a means to an individual's end and interest. The individual gives consent to create a sovereign state in order only to secure his self-interest – latter being the maintenance of peace and order, and the security of person and property. The task of maintaining the peace and order in the life of an individual is entrusted to the sovereign state only on the understanding that the latter would better serve the purpose than an individual could have by himself. The principle of individualism that is found pervasive in Hobbes also affects his conception of liberty and right. Shapiro clarifies it:

> A central and basic consequence of the Hobbesian view is that the private individual becomes the subject of all legitimate rights. At the most general level, Hobbes regards all moral assertions as meaningfully predicable only of individuals, and his science of morality is deduced from his theory of man in his natural state. The moral imperatives

> embedded in the laws of nature are rational imperatives for the survival of naturally private individuals.[2]

Even under the all-powerful sovereign state, Hobbes is concerned to secure the liberty and rights of the individual. While the liberty is licence in the state of nature, it is regulated by the laws in a political society. Law does not annihilate but only regulate individual's liberty of actions. Unlike in the state of nature, the liberty here is defined within the framework of the law of the state. However, he is free to enjoy liberty in his private sphere and in the spheres where the law is silent.

JOHN LOCKE

The principle of individualism culminates in Locke's philosophy of rights. He attaches supreme value to the individual by claiming for him certain innate and inviolable rights based on his pre-social nature. According to him, it is human individual in the mythical state of nature, who possesses such natural rights as the right to life, liberty and property prior to the formation of a political system. These rights inherently belong to the individual in the state of nature, and it is only for *more* effective protection of these rights than he can do in the state of nature that he gives consent for a political system. The primary concern for Locke remains to be safeguarding the natural rights of the individual, which he is supposed to enjoy in the state of nature. As a thoroughgoing individualist, Locke places individual's needs and interests in the form of rights before the state. The state is subordinate to the individual; it is a means to serve the individual's end, i.e. to safeguard his natural rights. States Shapiro:

> Locke believed, as did Hobbes, that the autonomous individual is the subject of all legitimate rights. He or she is the subject of all natural rights and all civil rights must

---

[2] I. Shapiro, *The Evolution of Rights in Liberal Theory*, Cambridge: Cambridge University Press, 1986, p. 59.

> ultimately be a function of his or her personal assent. Thus are churches and other religious bodies voluntary associations of individuals with no more substantial powers than the constituting members confer upon them. Thus, ultimately, is the private individual the author of the system of public law and the state itself.[3]

Thus the individual is the centre of all functions of the state. The state owes its origin in the individual's consent, and perpetuates its rule so long as it is capable of protecting the basic rights of the individual. Contrary to Hobbes, Locke bestows sovereignty to the individual rather than to the state. Locke even grants the individual the right to resist the state if it functions contrary to the law of nature, i.e. without regard for individual's natural and inalienable rights.

Unlike Hobbes, Locke is in favour of limited functions of the government. He rejects political absolutism in favour of political *laissez faire* which, according to him, would pave the way for better enjoyment of the rights of man. In Locke's scheme of rights, the liberty of the individual is not enjoyed within the limit set by the state but "within the bounds of the law of nature". That is to say, the limit to man's liberty is in the rights of others. The state has no authority to put limit to individual's liberty but only to maintain the *status quo* of the state of nature in respect of facilitating individual's enjoyment of natural rights. The life of the state depends on the efficient preservation of the individual's life, liberty and property. The state has nothing to do with all other dimensions of man, such as rational, moral or aesthetic, which he is at full liberty to develop.

THOMAS PAINE

Paine too advocates individualism in elaborating his views on the rights of man. Though his belief in the rights of man and

[3] I. Shapiro, *The Evolution of Rights in Liberal Theory*, pp. 122-23.

the principle of individualism associated with the idea is basically Lockean, he differs from Locke with regard to the details of these issues. Paine seems to be more careful than Locke to invest the individual with his rights and privileges within the framework of popular sovereignty. Norma Marshall points out:

> Paine placed greater stress on the complete equality of all individuals and on the right of all to participate in government or in choosing representatives. Paine also insisted on complete liberty in the exercise of individual rights; where Locke suggested that the State might limit religious freedom in order to preserve harmony and peace, Paine argued that the State had no legitimate power at all over the individual's religious beliefs.[4]

In contrast to Burke, Paine retains the Lockean premise that man's civil rights are rooted in natural rights, and it is only to have natural rights *better* secured that individual enters into a "social contract". But this contract does not mean submission of subjects to the will of a ruler but a contract of association among *equals*. And the only task of such a sovereign state is mutual protection of natural rights by the creation and administration of law. In Paine's words,

> Here then is the origin and rise of government; namely, a mode rendered necessary by the inability of moral virtue to govern the world; here too is the design and end of government, viz. freedom and security.[5]

Thus Paine reduces the role of government to a minimum and magnified the importance of society which is not artificial like government but natural in origin. For, it is

---

[4] N. Marshall, "Paine and the Rights of Man", in David Muschamp (ed.) *Political Thinkers*, London: Macmillan Education., 1986, p. 152.

[5] T. Paine, "Common Sense" in John Dos Passos (ed.) *The Living Thoughts of Tom Paine*, New Delhi: Rupa & Co., 2002, p. 67.

the society rather than the state, which is capable of attending to the diverse needs and interests of the individual. But as an ardent individualist, Paine emphasizes that the function of both state and society must be focused on safeguarding the rights of the individual.

For Paine, all rights belong originally and equally to the individual. But on entering the political system, he is capable of retaining some of these rights, such as the intellectual rights, the rights conducive to his own comfort and happiness, which he has the power to execute. But some other rights he has to subordinate to the social order. For, he lacks the natural power to exercise such rights as the right to security and protection, and this requires the collective support of civil society and government. But both kinds of rights are meant for serving the needs and interests of the individual.

It may be pointed out that the principle of individualism is not only associated with the natural-rights thinkers whom we have elaborated above, but it is a general trend of Western modernism. The Kantians and the Utilitarians too recognize the supreme value of the individual. The individuals are identified by the Kantians as rational and autonomous beings who are "ends in themselves", and they are possessed of intrinsic dignity and equal moral worth. The Utilitarian philosophers, such as Jeremy Bentham and J.S. Mill, have laid the foundation of their moral and political philosophy on individual human nature and psychology. They believe in fixed human nature. Pleasure is the ultimate object of desire, and it is the natural fact about a human individual. The consideration of pleasure and pain is the motivating force behind all human actions. It is the individual who will determine what action is morally right or wrong as it produces pleasure or pain. The good of society consists in "the greatest happiness of the greatest number". It is the individual's happiness that makes up the happiness of the society. Thus the individual is of ultimate value and compositional unit of the whole. That is, there is no entity called society but only the collection of individuals who compose it. Let us close the section by quoting from a recent individualist, Karl Popper. He writes:

> . . . all social phenomena, and especially the functioning of all social institutions, should always be understood as resulting from the decisions, actions, attitudes, etc., of human individuals, and that we should never be satisfied by an explanation in terms of so-called "collectives" (states, nations, races, etc.).[6]

In concluding the section, it may be said that the principle of individualism that has dominated the understanding of natural rights is only one trend among others. Alternative views are needed to be focused upon. The Confucianism and other Asian cultures, for example, lay stress on harmony and the value of community. Besides, there are group rights, namely, the rights of women and children. Rights of women and children are specific to them because of problems and needs that are peculiar to them. The idea of women's rights is first found in modern times in Mary Wollstonecraft's celebrated book *A Vindication of the Rights of Women*, published in 1792, in response to the promulgation of the natural rights-of-man theory. While describing woman's problems and issues, she portrays woman as *individual*. Similarly, children are also needed to be treated as group, for they have problems and needs that are peculiar to them. The natural rights thinkers have not paid attention to children's rights. The rights of the children include: right to family environment, right to parental care, rights against economic exploitation, right to protection against sexual abuse and exploitation, juvenile justice and so on. In these respects, the world-view on which the natural rights are based is not

[6] K. Popper, *The Open Society and Its Enemies*, vol. II, London: Routledge & Kegan Paul, repr., 1999, p. 98.

self-sufficient, and it is needed to be supplemented by other viewpoints.

Rationality

The second most important characteristic of the Western world-view is rationality or logical thinking of man. The rationality exerts immense influence upon all kinds of inquiry or research, be it scientific, social, or economic. It enjoys superiority over other forms of knowing truths. The Western modernism has firm belief in what is arrived as a result of careful and rigorous logical argument. Emotion or feeling has no role to play in rational-scientific knowledge in the objective and factual sense. What is the nature of rationality? Introducing himself as "the last laggard of the Enlightenment", Popper elaborates the sense in which the Enlightenment thinkers have taken to mean the term "rationality". He writes:

> Any reasonable person, and therefore, I hope, any rationalist, knows quite well that reason plays a very modest role in human life: it is the role of critical consideration, of critical discussion. What I mean when talking of reason or rationalism is nothing more than a conviction that we can learn through criticism, that is, through critical discussion with others and through self-criticism: that we can learn from our mistakes. A rationalist is a person who is willing to learn from others, not simply by accepting their opinions, but by allowing them to criticize his ideas and by criticizing theirs: in other words by critical discussion. The true rationalist does not believe that he or anyone else has a monopoly on wisdom. He knows very well that we constantly need new ideas and that criticism does not produce them. But he believes that criticism can help us to separate the wheat from the chaff. He is also aware of the fact that the rejection or acceptance of an idea can never be a purely rational matter. But only critical discussion can help us to see an idea from many sides and to judge it fairly.

> A rationalist will, of course, not assert that all human relations can be fully explored by critical discussion; that again would be most unreasonable. But a rationalist may perhaps point out that the attitude of give and take, which is at the bottom of critical discussion, is also of the greatest importance in purely human relations. For the rationalist will easily be able to see that he owes his rationality to other men.[7]

What this passage means is that the rationality is not the exclusive property of an individual but is constituted by the interaction with others. Rationality needs co-operation from others in terms of arguments. The truth is arrived at by consensus, and hence rationality here is meant to be "consensual" rationality which is advocated by the Enlightenment thinkers. That human beings are essentially rational animal is taken over by the modern Europe from the Greeks, and given supreme importance to it as the only source of knowledge, as a mode of critical thinking or argument, etc. As Popper rightly acknowledges that

> . . . our Western civilization is, historically speaking, largely a product of that rationalist mode of thought which our civilization has inherited from the Greeks.[8]

The strong belief in rationality or logical thinking of man is inextricably associated with the conception of natural rights. Human beings in this perspective are regarded as *essentially* rational. That is, the rationality is the natural and intrinsic characteristic of man, which makes him similar to his fellow-beings as well as distinguishes him from brutes. To be rational means various mental activities including the capacity to think abstractly. It is this characteristic of being rational that has been taken by the natural rights thinkers to be the defining

---

[7] K. Popper, "What Does the West Believe in?", in Karl Popper (ed.) *In Search of Better World*, London: Routledge, 1994, p. 205.

[8] Ibid., p. 209.

feature of man. Further, the law of nature within the bounds of which man is said to have led their life in the mythical state of nature, and from which the concept of natural rights is derived, is known by reason. Thus the natural rights thinkers take rationality or reason as the only source of knowledge or the only way of knowing the truth.

In modern times, Hobbes provides a distinctive role of reason in human life, though this role is subordinated by him to the demands of appetites and passions to ensure self-preservation. For him, reason helps choose the best means to self-preservation and satisfy his appetites. He understands reason in mathematical terms. Hobbes defines reason as

> nothing but *reckoning* (that is, adding and subtracting) of the consequences of general names agreed upon, for the *marking* and *signifying* of our thoughts; I say *marking* them, when we reckon by ourselves; and signifying, when we demonstrate, or approve our reckoning to other men.[9]

According to Hobbes, we find reason at work, for example, when we reckon "man" as being the combination of physical body, animalism and rationality. Despite the presence of rationality in man, according to Hobbes, he is always driven by his desires and passions.

On Locke's view, human reason stands for logical reason which distinguishes him from brutes as well as enables him to perceive what are right and wrong, liberty and equality, law and obligation. The law of nature, for Locke, is known by reason. Man not only knows the law of nature by means of reason but also guided by it to have his general good, i.e. to preserve his life, liberty and possessions. As Locke points out:

---

[9] T. Hobbes, *Leviathan*, ed. with an Introduction and Notes by J.C.A. Gaskin, Oxford: Oxford University Press, Oxford World's Classics, 2008, p. 28.

> The state of nature has a law of nature to govern it, which obliges everyone: and reason, which is that law, teaches all mankind, who will but consult it, that being all equal and independent; no one ought to harm another in his life, health, liberty, or possessions.[10]

Here Locke identifies law of nature with reason and has made the latter the basis of the equality of all men. It also enables him to play his part in God's design for the world. Reason is taken by Locke to be a natural capacity of human individuals. He acknowledges "an equal rational potential in all men" and this is evident from his following statement:

> God has been more beautiful to Mankind than so. He has given them a Mind that can reason without being instructed in Methods of Syllogizing: the Understanding is not taught to reason by these Rules; it has a native Faculty to perceive the Coherence, or Incoherence of its *Ideas*, and can range them right, without any such perplexing Repetitions.[11]

Following Locke, Paine too sees man as a rational creature, and this rationality of man, according to him, is not acquired by education but something inherent in his nature. He has firm faith on rational and enlightened human beings who are able to perceive the conveniences of social order, and to recognize the legitimacy of curtailing the individual, in favour of civil rights.

Among other Western philosophers, who emphasize reason or rationality, there are the utilitarians like Bentham and Mill. For both Bentham and Mill, reason is the capacity of individual to select the best means to fulfil his desires and passions. Human beings are conceived of by the utilitarians

---

10 J. Locke, *Two Treatises of Government*, ed. Mark Goldie, London: Everyman Edition, 1993, p. 117.

11 J. Locke, *An Essay Concerning Human Understanding*, Oxford: Oxford University Press, Oxford World's Classics, 2008, p. 436.

to be the rational creatures who are sole judges of what would give them pleasure, and determine what is morally right. The importance of rationality reaches its culminating stage in the philosophy of Kant, the last great philosopher of the Enlightenment. He lays the foundation of his entire philosophical enterprise on human reason. In his ethics in particular, he recognizes the dignity of the individual on the basis of human reason, and it is the latter which requires us to treat other human beings with dignity and equal moral worth, i.e. to respect them as "ends in themselves". It is again, for him, by the use of rational will that we can escape the tyranny of our inclinations, and guide our desires and passions.

In concluding the section, it may be noted that the recognition of rationality by the Enlightenment thinkers as the *only* way of knowledge is narrow in scope. For, it ignores a variety of other ways to get access to truths. Drama, music, intuition, love and such other expressions of emotion are all important ways through which we can "know" truths. Sri Aurobindo argues:

> The intellectual reason is not man's only means of knowledge. All action, all perception, all aesthesis and sensation, all impulse and will, all imagination and creation imply a universal, many-sided force of knowledge at work and each form or power of this knowledge has its own distinct nature and law, its own principle of order and arrangement, its logic proper to itself, and need not follow, still less be identical with the law of nature, order and arrangement which the intellectual reason would assign to it or itself follow if it had control of all these movements.[12]

The power of action and the aesthetic experience referred to in the passage enable man to realize the truth about himself

---

[12] Sri Aurobindo, *The Human Cycle*, Pondicherry: Sri Aurobindo Ashram, 3rd edn., 1998, pp. 103-04.

and his rights. The eminent examples of the power of action are provided by Nelson Mandela and Aung San Suu Kyi, who have fought for human rights and democracy in their own countries. The human rights discourse may derive their sustenance not only from drama, poetry or arts but also from localized moral discourses and the practices which are not necessarily of intellectual kind. Thus the Western emphasis on rational thinking as the only way of truth and communication is merely one of the many-sided forces of knowledge. Again, Sri Aurobindo asserts:

> The rational or intellectual man is not the last and highest ideal of manhood, nor would a rational society be the last and highest expression of the possibilities of an aggregate human life, – unless indeed we give to this word, reason, a wider meaning than it now possesses and include in it the combined wisdom of all our powers of knowledge, those which stand below and above the understanding and logical mind as well as this strictly rational part of our nature. The Spirit, that manifests itself in man and dominates secretly the phases of his development, is greater and profounder than his intellect and drives towards a perfection that cannot be shut in by the arbitrary constructions of the human reason.[13]

According to Sri Aurobindo, the intellect does not have access to the inmost truth of spirit. The knowledge attained through intellect is still incomplete and superficial, and it is needed to be supplemented by spiritual Self-knowledge that enables us to perceive our inmost self, to realize the Divinity within us, which deserves to be respected and honoured.

Swami Vivekananda, a nineteenth-century Indian thinker and activist, undermines the intellect and highlighted the role of feeling in human life. For him, the "heart" has primacy

---

[13] Sri Aurobindo, *The Human Cycle*, p. 114.

over intellect in moving and moulding the social and spiritual life of man. He writes:

> The intellect is only the street-cleaner, cleansing the path for us, a secondary worker, the policeman; but the policeman is not a positive necessity for the workings of society. He is only to stop disturbances, to check wrong-doing, and that is all the work required of the intellect.[14]

For Vivekananda, the intellect is blind, for it cannot move of itself. The feeling, and not the intellect, that enables a man to move forward and achieve the spiritual Self-knowledge. Indeed, the web of social relations is based on feeling, and it is the latter which prompts a man to work not only for the good of his fellow-beings but also for all beings in the world.

Conclusion

In this chapter, we have made an attempt to analyse the two prominent characteristics of the Western world-view that have shaped the formulation of the conception of natural rights – individualism and rationality. The natural rights thinkers, such as Hobbes, Locke and Paine have brought man as *individual* into focus and conceive rights that belong to *individual*. While Hobbes portrays man as completely ego-centric, isolated and solitary being possessed of what he calls "the right of nature", Locke and Paine place individual's needs and interests in the form of rights before the state. But, in our view, the notion of individualism ignores the social nature of men, and their possession of rights as social beings. For example, the rights of women and children are specific to them, and these are group-rights. Second, Hobbes admits the role of reason in human life but he subordinates reason to the demands of appetites and passions to ensure self-preservation. For him,

---

14 *The Complete Works of Swami Vivekananda*, Calcutta: Advaita Ashrama, Mayavati Memorial Edition, 1992, vol. II, p. 306.

reason enables man to choose suitable means to self-preservation. Locke recognizes a greater role of reason or rationality in human life. For him, reason enables man to distinguish between right and wrong, law and obligation. The law of nature is known by reason and guides man to preserve his life, liberty and possession. But this rationalistic tradition, in our view, suffers from inadequacy as it does not recognize other modes of knowing truths, such as music, drama, intuition and love. Indian thinkers like Sri Aurobindo and Swami Vivekananda lay stress on human *feelings* as an important source of knowledge.

6

Human Rights

Inventing New Dimensions

It was total departure from the natural-rights tradition when in later half of the nineteenth century some philosophers began to develop theories of human rights. This trend of developing human-rights theories independently of the natural-rights paradigm continues till recent times, although the influence of the natural-rights thinking on the contemporary analysis of rights is not totally done away with. These philosophical theories of rights increasingly become free of the world-view that has shaped the theories of natural rights. The theories of natural rights are replaced by the theories of *human* rights. It was T.H. Green who first put forward a radical critique of natural rights and elaborated his own views on the concept of rights. Again, after the adoption of the UN Declaration of Human Rights, 1948, many contemporary philosophers joined this chorus in their own unique ways to develop the theories of human rights. In the present chapter we would consider the theories of rights developed by T.H. Green, Margaret MacDonald, Carl Wellman, Joel Feinberg and Rex Martin. These thinkers invented various new dimensions of human rights from their respective perspectives.

Rights as Recognized Claims

The nineteenth-century British political thought was dominated by the two contrasting doctrines – utilitarianism and idealism. Though both the theories seem to concern themselves with a common issue, namely, the individual liberty, they differ in their method and approach to the matter. Individual liberty under the patronage of the utilitarians was a popular creed. In their zeal to safeguard the individual liberty the utilitarians developed somewhat negative attitude towards the authority of the state. In his *On Liberty*, J.S. Mill argues that those conducts of individual which affect himself alone, the state has no excuse for intervening in his affairs. T.H. Green, as a member of the idealist camp, finds it as his task to revive the confidence in the authority of the state without impairing the ideal of individual liberty. He makes an attempt to strike a balance between the individual liberty and the authority of the state. And in doing so, he gives a pivotal role to rights in his writings.

Green puts forward some arguments against the natural-rights doctrine in the context of evaluating the views of Hobbes, Spinoza, Locke, Rousseau and Austin, although it has already been severely assailed by Bentham and his fellow utilitarians. He rejects the doctrine of natural rights on three grounds:

1. The doctrine assumes that these rights have been brought into society from a pre-social state of human life,
2. yet this doctrine insists that these rights can be held against society, and
3. it also asserts that an individual is entitled to enjoy these rights without regard for his duties that he owes to the society.[1]

Green is primarily concerned with moral rights, i.e. the rights that are justified on moral grounds. Like Mill, Green

---

[1] M. Freeden, *Rights*, Delhi: World View Publications, 1998, p. 20.

cannot conceive of individual as one who enjoys his life in solitary orbit of self-regarding activities, in isolation from his fellow beings. For him, individuals are social beings, and it is only as part of social nexus that they have rights. But society is not conceived by Green as the sum-total of discreet and isolated individuals but is united by a conception of the common good which an individual is able to recognize as a member of the society as his ideal good. Hence Green writes:

> No one therefore can have a right except (1) as a member of a society, and (2) of a society in which some common good is recognized by the members of the society as their own ideal good, as that which should be for each of them. The capacity for being determined by a good so recognized is what constitutes personality in the ethical sense; and for this reason there is truth in saying that only among persons, in the ethical sense, can there come to be rights.[2]

What Green clarifies in the passage is that rights cannot belong to man merely as individual but as social being, provided that he can recognize in that common good an ideal good which is same for himself and for others as well. Green believes in the primacy of self-realization for which an individual is required to pursue a common good as a member of the society. This conception of self as the good to be realized and its pursuits can take place only within a social context. For, a man is able to realize his potentialities only in community with others towards a common good.

Conversely, when a person is capable of being determined by the conception of a common good, he can be said to possess rights. As a social being, a person *ought* to possess rights, which

> expresses the relation of man to an end conceived as absolutely good, to an end which, whether desired or not, is

[2] T.H. Green, *Lectures on the Principles of Political Obligation*, New Delhi: Orient Longman, 1967, p. 44.

> conceived as intrinsically desirable. The moral capacity implies a consciousness on the part of the subject of the capacity that its realization is an end desirable in itself, and rights are the condition of realizing it.[3]

In other words, the possession of rights relates a person to an end which is not valid for some *other* end considered valuable but something that has an absolute worth. And the common good as an end has an absolute worth and is, for Green, intrinsically desirable, that is, desirable in itself. Rights are the conditions for realizing this end having absolute worth. Rights are claimed for making the common good a reality in the life of man by providing a power to him. Further, rights enable a person to freely exercise his power and thereby to secure the treatment of one person by another on equal footing. But in doing so, each person should realize that the free exercise of his power depends on allowing the free exercise of power of every other member of the society.

The point that is central to Green's scheme of rights is the idea of common good. It is the concept of common good on the basis of which Green analyses the condition necessary to the realization of human potentialities and the extent to which the state could be used to pave the way for the pursuit of self-perfection. The common good is conceived as an ideal not yet attained by the individual; it is "the absolute end" of man as a social being. The ideal of common good enables a person to recognize his power as a right leading to the growth and development of his potentialities. Hence a right is

> a power of which the exercise by the individual or by some body of men is recognized by a society, either as itself directly essential to a common good, or as conferred by an authority of which the maintenance is recognized as so essential.[4]

---

[3] T.H. Green, *Lectures on the Principles of Political Obligation*, pp. 44-45.

[4] Ibid., p. 113.

Green holds the view that right is a power exercised by person and recognized by society as essential for the realization of the common good. He is reluctant to use the term "natural" in the context of rights, in the sense that they actually exist when a man is born and continue to exist as long as human race. For Green, rights can be "natural" only in the sense that they would apply to fulfilling "a moral capacity without which a man would not be a man".[5] In other words, rights are "necessary to the end which it is the vocation of human society to realize".[6]

One of the reasons for Green to repudiate the doctrine of natural rights, as we have already pointed out, is that it de-links rights from duties that individual owes to his society. He says:

> Because a group of beings are capable each of conceiving an absolute good of himself and of conceiving it to be good for himself as identical with, and because identical with, the good of the rest of the group, there arises for each a consciousness that the common good should be the object of action, i.e. a duty, and a claim in each to a power of action that shall be at once secured and regulated by the consciousness of a common good on the part of the rest, i.e. a right.[7]

In other words, as a moral being I have a capacity for duty towards the realization of the common good, and in order to fulfil my duty I should have a right – the latter being the condition for fulfilling my duty. Green points out that although all rights here are taken as relative to moral ends or duties, this must not be confused with the popular assertion that every right implies a duty, or that right and duty are correlative. In this context, the correlativity of right and duty is accepted, in the sense that the

[5] T.H. Green, *Lectures on the Principles of Political Obligation*, p. 47.

[6] Ibid., p. 34.

[7] Ibid., pp. 47-48.

> possession of a right by any person both implies an obligation on the part of someone else, and is conditional upon the recognition of certain obligations on the part of the person possessing it.[8]

What is meant here is that the fulfilment of man's vocation as a moral being is his basic duty, and this duty cannot be carried out except through the exercise of rights.

According to Green, any right contains two aspects: on the one hand, it is a claim of the individual, and the recognition of it by the society on the other. Green writes:

> In analysing the nature of any right, we may conveniently look at it on two sides, and consider it as on the one hand a claim of the individual, arising out of his rational nature, to the free exercise of some faculty; on the other, as a concession of that claim by society, a power given by it to the individual of the putting the claim in force.[9]

A person claims certain rights which are more or less articulate and pronounced for the development of his moral personality. For, the moral personality can be developed only through the exercise of rights, i.e. "through the recognition by members of a society of powers in each other contributory to a common good, and the regulation of those powers by that recognition".[10] This claim arises out of his rational nature because of the free exercise of some faculty. But this claim would remain merely a claim unless it is conceded by other members of the society. When the claim made by the individual is co-ordinate with the recognition of the claim by others, only then there exists a right. An individual's moral capacity to identify his ideal good in the common good and to regulate the exercise of his power concerning the good that others recognize are what make it

---

[8] T.H. Green, *Lectures on the Principles of Political Obligation*, p. 41.

[9] Ibid., p. 144.

[10] Ibid., p. 45.

obligatory to have rights. In order to exercise a right it is not enough to have a claim of the individual but this claim has to be recognized by the members of the society.[11] A claim of the individual is put into force only when it is recognized by others. Thus moral personality can be developed only through the two-faceted rights, and thereby it would be contributory to the common good. But these two distinguishable aspects, Green says, belong to the same common consciousness.[12]

Now, the question is: Why rights are so crucial for the person as a moral and social being? Green's reply is that "a right is a power claimed and recognized as contributory to a common good".[13] In other words, rights are necessary in the life of a person for his development and thereby to realize his end as a moral being – the end that is absolute and intrinsically desirable. Green seems to argue that although an individual has rights only as a social being, the focal point of growth and development is *not* the social group but the individual. It is for the self-development of the individual that rights are invoked in social life, although political and social contexts are not without significance. Paul Harris and John Morrow write:

---

11 Elsewhere Green says, "There can be no right without a consciousness of common interest on the part of members of a society. Without this there might be certain powers on the part of individuals, but no recognition of these powers by others as powers of which they allow the exercise, nor any claim to such recognition, and without this recognition or claim to recognition there can be no right." See T.H. Green's *Lectures on the Principles of Political Obligation*, p. 48.

12 As Amal Kumar Mukhopadhyay clarifies, "In all this discussion the main thesis Green tries to establish is that the origin of right lies both inside and outside the individual. On the one hand, it flows from his moral personality. On the other, it is derived from social relations." See his *The Ethics of Obedience: A Study of the Philosophy of T.H. Green*, Calcutta: The World Press, 1967, p. 112.

13 T.H. Green, *Lectures on the Principles of Political Obligation*, p. 110.

> Green argues that the essential social dimension to individual self-realization means that the individual must regard social institutions and practices (political organization, customs, mores, law) as collective efforts after a common good. They are the result of the need to secure and maintain the conditions within which individuals can pursue their self-realization in their own ways, and of the need to harmonize the ways in which they do so. As such, these institutions and practices need to be acknowledged by the individual as deserving his allegiance and consideration as essential to his own self-realization – provided they continue to act as means to the common good and not as impediments to it.[14]

Further, Green points out that rights cannot be held against society and state; they are only sustainer and harmonizer of social relations on which all rights are founded.

Rights as Taking a Stand

In her article "Natural Rights", Margaret MacDonald has levelled some specific and pointed criticisms against the traditional doctrine of natural rights, but her criticisms move along sympathetic lines. In the last section of the essay, she puts forward her own views on rights. Her article

> while in the broad stream of what is sometimes called "analytic philosophy" is near in spirit to the Logical Positivism of the 1930s than to the linguistic or conceptual analysis of the post-war years.[15]

She is concerned here to understand the nature of propositions/assertions expressing right-claims and to classify

---

[14] P. Harries and J. Morrow, "Introduction", *Lectures on the Principles of Political Obligation and Other Writings*, Cambridge: Cambridge University Press, 1986, pp. 6-7.

[15] A.J.M. Milne, *Freedom and Rights: A Philosophical Synthesis*, New York: George Allen & Unwin, 1968, p. 57.

them into one of the following three types among indefinite number of utterances. These are:

1. Tautological or analytical propositions,
2. empirical or contingent propositions, and
3. assertions of value.

She makes an attempt in this article to show that some of the difficulties we face with the doctrine of natural rights is because of confusions of propositions about them either with analytical or with empirical propositions, whereas the assertions concerning right-claims, according to MacDonald, are ethical assertions.

Though MacDonald has directed a few specific points of criticism against some of the premises of the doctrine of natural rights, she has not entirely dismissed it as a tissue of confusions. She says:

> The exponents of the natural Rights of Man were trying to express what they deemed to be the fundamental conditions of *human* social life and government. And it is by the observance of some such conditions, I suggest, that human societies are distinguished from anthills and beehives.[16]

She further points out that the natural rights of man conceived by its exponents *independently* of civil society and government in order to lay stress on their fundamental nature, i.e. to lay emphasis on the natural rights of man as the ultimate moral and social values without observation of which human society would no longer remain fit for human survival. These are the conditions of a good society. But these conditions are *not* given by Nature as the latter cannot dictate what ought we to do. For MacDonald, Nature as such does not harbour values to provide directions to human beings in their social and political

---

16 M. MacDonald, "Natural Rights", in Jeremy Waldron (ed.) *Theories of Rights*, Oxford: Oxford University Press, 1984, p. 33.

life. It is man who determines standards through his choices and preferences independently of Nature. As she writes:

> In short, "natural rights" are the conditions of a good society. But what those conditions are is not given by nature or mystically bound up with the essence of man and his inevitable goal, but is determined by human decisions.[17]

Among the three types of human utterances mentioned above, assertions about natural rights, according to MacDonald, fall within the third category mentioned above. That is, utterances about natural rights are neither tautological or analytical nor empirical or contingent but are value-assertions which "include all those which result from human choice and preference, for example in art and personal relations, as well as in morals and politics".[18] Now, what are the characteristics of value-assertions? According to MacDonald, an important feature of such assertions is that they are "more like records of *decisions* than propositions".[19] For her:

> To assert that "Freedom is better than slavery" or "All men are of equal worth" is not to state a fact but to *choose* a side. It announces *This is where I stand*.[20]

The point here is that utterances that concern ultimate social values like human rights are *decisions*, rather than propositions, as a result of human choices and preferences. They do not state facts but are meant to take a stand or to choose a side. While taking a decision, one has to choose a side with regard to certain ultimate social values, for example, whether we prefer freedom or slavery.[21] Thus decisions which concern the

---

17 M. MacDonald, "Natural Rights", in *Theories of Rights*, p. 34.

18 Ibid., p. 34.

19 Ibid., p. 35.

20 Ibid.

21 As MacDonald writes, "Lawyers and art critics are not frauds, but neither are they scientists. They are more like artists who use material →

ultimate structure of society are more like choosing our favourite poems, novels, pictures, etc. but not like choosing to accept the law of gravitation. In fact, one can*not* choose to accept the scientific law like the law of gravitation but rather he is bound to accept it. In case of choosing this or that novel, one is at liberty. Here, two important characteristics of such decisions are to be noted.

First, the decisions about fundamental values of society are neither *explicit* decisions nor taken at a particular date. These decisions come from those people who live and work in society and take part in operating its institutions. Second, these decisions are not taken on the basis of any evidence. MacDonald considers the doctrine of equality according to which all human beings are to be treated as of equal worth. But on what ground the equality has to be accorded to men? According to the natural rights theorists, it is having reason as a natural fact that provides the ground for equal treatment of all human beings. That is, the decision here is taken on the basis of possessing by men a natural characteristic called "reason". Now a question arises: If in course of time a person no longer remains in possession of the natural characteristic called reason and becomes lunatic, then can the decision about treating him as having equal worth like other human beings hold true? Is the lunatic entitled any longer to claim his natural rights? MacDonald's reply to such a query is that losing rationality does not make him a mere animal. He is very well entitled to his human rights even though he has lost his rationality. Thus reason or any *one* natural characteristic cannot be the basis of the value-assertion that all men are of equal

→ with results which impress and convince but do not *prove*. There is no conceivable method of *proving* that Keats is a better poet than Crabbe or that freedom is better than slavery. For assertions of value cannot be subjected to demonstrative or inductive methods." See her "Natural Rights", in *Theories of Rights*, p. 39.

worth. Now, does it follow then that the decision concerning the equal worth of human beings is arbitrary? MacDonald answers this question in the negative. She argues that although any evidence cannot be adduced (as we do in the case of a scientific law, such as the law of gravitation) in support of decisions concerning the ultimate social values, but they can be supported and defended in the way a lawyer defends his clients or a literary critic of his judgement that one poet is better than another.

To elaborate her position, MacDonald considers the situation that arises in a court room. The statements of the fact of certain case is known to both the prosecuting and defending lawyers, and the presentation of the statements of facts before the jury is not enough for winning the case. What is needed by the defending lawyer is to marshal those facts in a manner that would go to favour his client. His presentation involves not mere stating the facts but his voice, gesture, etc. all of which are supposed to influence the decision of the jury on his client's favour. It is in the like manner that the decision, which concerns the rights of man to liberty and equality, can be supported and defended but cannot be proved by evidence. MacDonald concludes:

> There are no certainties in the field of values. For there are no true or false beliefs about values, but only better or worse decisions and choices. And to encourage the better decisions we need to employ devices which are artistic rather than scientific. For our aim is not intellectual assent, but practical effects. These are not, of course, absolutely separate, for intellectual assent to a proposition or theory is followed by using it. But values, I think, concern only behaviour. They are not known, but accepted and acted upon.[22]

[22] M. MacDonald, "Natural Rights", in *Theories of Rights*, pp. 39-40.

The crux of MacDonald's arguments is as follows: According to natural-rights theorists, the law of nature and natural rights are standards by which existing human conditions are judged, and this standard is known by reason which is regarded as intrinsic property of man. But MacDonald argues that the characteristic of being rational is simply an empirical fact which does not constitute man's specific nature, and hence cannot set the standard of what ought to be. According to her, they cannot be known by reason as the latter is capable of knowing only analytic or tautological propositions. The assertions which concern natural law and natural rights, according to MacDonald, are neither analytic nor empirical propositions but are ethical assertions. The latter are records of decisions as a result of human choices and preferences that can*not* be proved but can only be defended in the way a lawyer defends his client or a literary critic defends a particular poet. A good counsel or a literary critic does *not* prove anything as a result of his arguments but uses his materials with results in order to impress and convince the jury. Similarly, the assertions of equality and liberty being in the nature of ethical assertions cannot be demonstrated by any inductive means but can only be decided and defended.

Rights as Constellations of Hohfeldian Elements

Wellman in his article "A New Conception of Human Rights" develops the idea that rights are constituted by a group of normative elements identified by Wesley Hohfeld in legal terms during the first quarter of the twentieth century. According to Hohfeld, legal rights could be constituted by any of the four elements – a liberty, a claim, a power, or an immunity. But he regards the claim-rights as a pre-eminent type of right among the four elements. Wellman agrees with Hohfeld that any of these four elements may be fundamental to a given right, but he does not think that each right is constituted by just the one element. For Wellman, every right is a complex normative structure, which typically involves several of these elements. Let us now briefly explain Hohfeld's conception of a legal right consisting of four elements, each element having a unique second-party correlative.

A legal *liberty* to do *A* – which consists in the absence of duty on the agent's part to refrain from *A* – is matched with other people's lack of a claim that *A* not be done by the agent. For example, I am at liberty to purchase a car of Maruti company in that I have no duty not to, and others have no claim against me not to. A legal *claim* correlates with a legal duty of some second party. A legal *power* to do *A* consists in a person's legal competence to perform an act which will create, or at least bring to bear, certain legal consequences for a second party and is matched by a liability to be acted on. For example, a policeman has the legal power over fleeing suspect to place him under arrest and the suspect is liable to be arrested by the police. And a person's *immunity* from *A* is necessarily correlated with a lack of power on the part of others to do *A*, and thus the correlative of an immunity is a disability. For example, I have legal immunity against others when I practise the religion of my choice.

Since Wellman thinks that the problem of defining the content of rights has been better solved by law than ethics, he takes legal rights as his model of human rights. He finds it particularly helpful to define the content of legal rights following the Hohfeldian terminology that explicates them in unambiguous and practical terms. Wellman intends to preserve all the four features, defined by Hohfeld, in his 'new' conception of human rights. The Hohfeldian conception of a legal right is not an aggregate of disparate legal liberties, claims, powers and immunities but a *cluster* of all these four features. Wellman conceives an analogous concept of ethical right as a complex system of ethical advantages, a cluster of ethical liberties, claims, powers and immunities as follows.

First, *X* has an ethical liberty to do *A* if and only if *X* does not have any duty not to do *A*. Here duty is taken to be based on some specific moral reason and need not be a duty *to* any determinate second party. I am at liberty to spend my spare cash as I wish or to practise any religion of my choice. Second, *X* has an ethical claim against *Y* that *Y* performs some action *A* if and only if *Y* has a duty to *X* to do *A*. For example, you have an ethical claim against me that I refrain from striking you or my child has an ethical claim against me that I support him. Here, the duty is a duty to someone who would be seriously injured by its non-performance. Third, *X* has the ethical power to bring about some ethical consequence *C* if and only if *X* possesses the competence required for performing some act with this ethical consequence. For example, I have the ethical power of making a promise, and this act not only creates an obligation to do what I have promised but also empowers the promisee to release me from my promise if he so chooses. By the term "competence" in the definition, Wellman refers to the qualifications or characteristics one must possess in order that one's action can actually bring about some sort of ethical consequence. Thus everyone is not competent to make promise or to release the promiser. Fourth, *X* is immune from some specified ethical consequence *C* if and only if there is no other party who is competent to do some action with this ethical consequence. For example, I am immune from the loss through any act of another of my ethical claim against second parties that they refrain from striking me.

According to Wellman, just as a legal right is a complex system of legal advantages, so an ethical right is a complex system of ethical advantages consisting of liberties, claims, powers, or immunities. What give these four constituents a unity is its core. Each and every right has a core which defines the essential content of a right. In other words, it is the defining core that holds together the constituent elements of a right. The defining core of my right to be repaid is my ethical claim to repayment. The essential content or defining core of my right to free speech is my ethical liberty of speaking out on controversial issues. The same defining core lies at the centre of my every power-right or immunity-right. Wellman writes:

> When we classify rights as claim-, power- or immunity-rights, it is to their defining cores that we refer. Whatever other legal elements may be contained in any right, they belong to this right because of their relation to its core. Thus, a legal right is not a mere aggregate or collection of disparate legal liberties, claims, powers and immunities; it is a system of legal advantages tied to its defining core.[23]

Just as there is a system of legal advantages tied to its defining core, so there is a cluster of ethical advantages integrated with their essential content. It is the defining core or essential content that gives stability to an ethical right and also maintains its unity even when its associated elements are changing. Thus Wellman distinguishes between the *defining* core and the *associated* elements in his conception of an ethical right. For example, the creditor's right to repayment includes not only a defining core, the *claim* against the debtor for repayment, but also a *liberty* to request or not to request for repayment, and a *power* to waive the repayment, and an *immunity* to be protected from arbitrary or wilful cancellation of the indebtedness.

Now, Wellman distinguishes human rights from other ethical rights. The right of a promisee, a teacher, or a citizen is not a human right, for they are not the right one has simply by virtue of being human. Traditionally, human rights are

---

23 C. Wellman, "A New Conception of Human Rights", in Morton E. Winston (ed.) *The Philosophy of Human Rights*, Belmont: Wadsworth Publishing Company, 1989, p. 90.

generally defined as those ethical rights that every human being possesses by virtue of being human. Wellman proposes a narrower conception of human rights which is as follows:

> I define a human right as an ethical right of the individual as human being vis-à-vis the state.[24]

In this definition, Wellman excludes other individual or organization as an addressee of human rights. He adduces two reasons in support of his exclusion of other individual or organization:

1. In his definition Wellman thinks it appropriate to follow the major human-rights documents which proclaim the state as the addressee of human rights; and
2. he finds the ethical relation of the individual human being to other individual or organization is quite different from his ethical relation to the state in that the latter has a much more greater role in human affairs.

In order to mark the distinctive role of the state Wellman proposes to reserve "the expression 'human right' to refer to a right any individual has *as* a human being *in face of* the state".[25] Hence, Wellman provides his final definition of human rights as follows:

> A human right is a cluster of ethical liberties, claims, powers and immunities that together constitute a system of ethical autonomy possessed by an individual as a human being vis-à-vis the state.[26]

Wellman now turns to illustrate his "new" conception of human rights with respect to the right to privacy. The term

---

[24] C. Wellman, "A New Conception of Human Rights", *The Philosophy of Human Rights*, p. 93.

[25] Ibid.

[26] Ibid.

"privacy" is opposite of being public. That is, it is a condition which is not open to public. Generally, it is regarded as unethical to invade one's private realm. Every human being requires privacy in his home, family, personal correspondence, etc. This also includes some relationships such as those between husband and wife, and doctor and patient. One is in need of privacy in these and other areas of human life for the development of his personality, for his sense of security and for the maintenance of certain sensitive relationships. Thus the privacy is considered to be an important good, which ought to be protected with respect to all persons. Wellman finds out three distinct elements in the right to privacy as its defining core or essential content: "a claim to freedom from invasions of one's privacy", "a claim to legal protection from invasions of one's privacy by the state or other individuals", and "the ethical claim of the individual against the state that it sustains the conditions necessary for the existence of privacy for the individual".[27] Wellman also brings out some associated ethical elements which contribute to the satisfaction of the three defining core of the right to privacy. The illustration of the right to privacy with respect to his "new" conception of human rights, Wellman hopes, would pave the way for similar analyses to be given for other human rights.

Rights as Claims

Feinberg begins his analysis of the nature of rights by means of a thought-experiment. He imagines a land called Nowheresville which is just like our own world except that no one in it has any rights. But the denizens of Nowheresville possess other moral qualities in abundance: they are benevolent, compassionate, sympathetic and deserving of the benefits of modern civilization. But it remains that they lack

[27] C. Wellman, "A New Conception of Human Rights", in *The Philosophy of Human Rights*, p. 93.

the power to claim something as their due. That is, they cannot claim *to* something and *against* someone else, which is based on some system of rules – be it legal or moral.

For Feinberg, rights are claims, and what are called claim-rights are traditionally distinguished by legal writers from liberties, immunities and powers with which they are often confused. In case of legal claim-rights, rights logically entail other person's duties. One example of such rights is the creditor's right to be paid by his debtor. Here, the creditor's right against his debtor and the debtor's duty to his creditor are but the same relation viewed from two different standpoints. But Feinberg argues for the primacy of claims over duties. If Nip has a claim-right against Tuck, then this implies that Tuck is bound by some duty to Nip who is free. The duties derivative from claims is missing in Nowheresville, for the denizens of the land lack the power to claim.

In order to establish his view that right is a sort of claim, Feinberg finds it feasible to explain the idea of a claim in informal analysis rather than by means of a formal definition. For him, one can learn more about what a claim is by attending to the activity of claiming. He begins by pointing out that "*claiming* is an elaborate sort of rule-governed *activity*. A claim is that which is claimed, the object of the act of claiming. . . ."[28] He distinguishes between (i) making claim to . . . , (ii) claiming that . . . , and having a claim. First of all, the activity of claiming involves "making claim to something". A claim is an activity in which individuals demand things as their due. For example, when an insurance policyholder places a demand to the insurance authority by presenting his policy deed to pay him the amount of money which is his due or an inventor stakes a claim for his patent right; these are the claims of the insurance

---

[28] J. Feinberg, "The Nature and Value of Rights", in *The Philosophy of Human Rights*, p. 68.

policyholder or an inventor. Thus only the individual who has a title to something, or who has qualified for it, can make a claim as a matter of right. What is distinctive about rights is that they can be claimed only by those who have already possessed them. In legal sense, "making claim to" means that the thing claimed is bound to happen. This is, for Feinberg, the "performative sense" of term "claim".

Feinberg now turns to the second employment of the term "claim", namely, "claiming that". Claiming that one has a right is to make an assertion that one is possessed of a certain right and to demand that it be recognized. This is what is called by Feinberg "the propositional claiming" as opposed to "performative claiming". In propositional claiming, it is not enough to make assertion of a claim but to make it listen to by those concerned. In other words, in case of "claiming that", to assert that something is the case goes together with the demand that it is to be recognized. In order to ensure that the demand is to be recognized, it is to be asserted under "appropriate circumstances" which may include when one is challenged or when one's possession of something is denied or acknowledged. Thus "having a right" is to be in a position to making a claim. Feinberg writes:

> Having rights, of course, makes claiming possible; but it is claiming that gives rights their special moral significance. . . . Having rights enables us to "stand up like men", to look others in the eye, and to feel in some fundamental way the equal of anyone. To think of oneself as the holder of rights is not to be unduly but properly proud, to have that minimal self-respect that is necessary to be worthy of the love and esteem of others. Indeed . . . what is called "human dignity" may simply be the recognizable capacity to assert claims.[29]

---

[29] J. Feinberg, "The Nature and Value of Rights", in *The Philosophy of Human Rights*, pp. 69-70.

Feinberg also analyses the third component involving the term "claim". Here, his question is: "what is to have a claim and how is this related to rights?" Feinberg replies that

> . . . having a claim consists in being in a position to claim, that is, to make claim to or claim that.[30]

This suggests that it is primarily a verbal rather than a normative activity. As the claim is an activity, it is quite different from *things*, such as coins, pens, pencils and other material possessions. Even the title in the form of tickets, certificates, receipts, etc. is not the same thing as the claim. The title is rather the evidence that establishes the claim as valid. According to this view, there may be a claim without ever claiming that to which one is entitled or even without being aware that one has the claim. Because one might be unaware of the fact that one is in a position to claim or might not be inclined to take the opportunity of that position for any reason, such as the fear that the government machinery is not working or debased and will not give effect to the valid claim of an individual.

On Feinberg's view, rights are not mere claims but *valid* claims. He rejects the view according to which all claims as such are valid and hence it is superfluous to use the adjective "valid" before the term "claim". He argues that all claims are *presented* as valid whether they are in fact valid or not. Only those claims, which are *in fact* valid, are acknowledged as rights. Hence Feinberg admits that there *are* certain claims which are *not* valid; these claims are merely *presented* as valid.[31]

---

30 J. Feinberg, "The Nature and Value of Rights", in *The Philosophy of Human Rights*, p. 70.

31 Feinberg writes, "Nearly all writers maintain that there is some intimate connection between having a claim and having a right. Some identify right and claim without qualification; some define 'right' as justified or justifiable claim, others as recognized claim, still others as valid claim. My own preference is for the latter definition". See his "The Nature and Value of Rights", in *The Philosophy of Human Rights*, p. 70.

In a parallel to the *prima facie* case in the judiciary, there may be *prima facie* sense of "claim". In the judiciary the initial evidence, which is put forward by a plaintiff is serious but not conclusive, is called *prima facie* case. Similarly, there may be *prima facie* case of a claim but not amounting to a right.

In Feinberg's view, if someone has a right, then this implies that he has a claim *to* something and *against* someone else. He writes:

> A man has a moral right when he has a claim the recognition of which is called for – not (necessarily) by legal rules – but by moral principles, or the principles of an enlightened conscience.[32]

In other words, there must be a set of reasons based on legal rules or moral principles to support a person's claim *to* something and *against* someone. But there may be someone having claim-to without knowing whom that claim-to might be against. Imagine a hungry and sickly orphan child living in a slum. Does not this child have a *claim* to be fed, taken care of and taught to be read? In Feinberg's view, a valid claim calls for, but does not entail, the duties of other person to satisfy the claim. If it is practicable for a claim to be satisfied, then it is enough justification for calling on relevant duties of determinate persons.

Thus in Feinberg's theory, a right is always a combination of two elements – a valid claim *to* something and *against* someone – although any of these two elements may be more clearly perceived in a particular case. He, however, speaks of special "manifesto sense" of right, which lacks addressee. "Natural needs", Feinberg analyses,

> are real claims if only upon hypothetical future beings not yet in existence. I accept the moral principle that to have an

---

32 J. Feinberg, "The Nature and Value of Rights", *The Philosophy of Human Rights*, p. 72.

> unfulfilled need is to have a kind of claim against the world, even if against no one in particular. A natural need for some good as such, like a natural desert, is always a reason in support of a claim to that good. A person in need, then, is always "in a position" to make a claim, even when there is no one in the corresponding position to do anything about it. Such claims, based on need alone, are "permanent possibilities of rights", the natural seed from which rights grow.[33]

The manifesto rights are a special class of rights, in the sense that they are based only on the validation of claims-to but a full-fledged right requires the combination of a valid claim-*to* with a claim-*against*, which are justified under a system of valid rules.

Rights as Recognized Entitlements

Rex Martin, in his paper "Human Rights and Civil Rights", presents rights as recognized entitlements. He begins by pointing out what is lacking in Feinberg's account of rights as valid claims. For Feinberg, rights are combination of two distinct dimensions: (i) they are claims-*to* something, and (ii) they are claims-*against* someone. In other words, rights are claims for entitlements, and they call for duties of other people in the fulfilment of that which is claimed. Human rights as valid claims fundamentally mean that the thing claimed is morally approved. It is for this reason that human rights are generally regarded as moral rights. But in order to be relevantly valid, human rights include some other factors, such as the thing claimed must be endorsed for *all* persons, the thing can be put into practice and able to provide justifiable ground for calling on duties of other people. The other main dimension, i.e. the claims-*against* requires that there must be relevant duties to be done by individuals. Human rights cannot

---

33 J. Feinberg "The Nature and Value of Rights", in *The Philosophy of Human Rights*, p. 72.

be fully valid claims, according to Feinberg, unless these two dimensions are combined together. What is distinctive of this account of human rights is that they are valid claims even though they are not responded to or recognized by governmental or individual courses of actions.

It is here that Martin finds a serious lacuna in Feinberg's account of rights. He writes:

> A valid claim can exist solely in the domain of moral argument but that which satisfies the claim cannot. It cannot because what satisfies the claim is the maintenance of a course of action and such maintenance is not confined to the realm of argument.[34]

Martin in his article is in search of that course of action, which satisfies the valid claims in order to be elevated to the status of human rights. Martin tells us to imagine the case of travel as morally valid claim. We can conceive travel as a morally valid claim by distinguishing it from emigration, by excluding the obvious cases of unlawful travel, by prohibiting travel for reasons of public health or war and so on. Thus the liberty to travel as an innocent activity finds a place in men's reflective consciousness as a human right, which is morally decisive and well-grounded. And the relevant duties of other people are in place for the fulfilling that morally valid claim. But despite widespread moral assent the liberty to travel, according to Martin, cannot be elevated to the status of a human right *due to lack of maintenance of an appropriate course of action*. Martin writes:

> The right to travel would be vitiated *as a right* if it were not enforced or promoted at all. In such a case the right is a merely nominal one, a right that existed in name only but not in fact. A nominal right is in principle never an

[34] R. Martin, "Human Rights and Civil Rights", in *The Philosophy of Human Rights*, p. 76.

> enforceable one; enforcement simply does not belong to its nature.[35]

It remains as "right only on paper and nowhere else".[36] Even as the liberty to travel is recognized as valid claim from moral point of view it has failed to be a right due to lack of an appropriate course of action. So a morally valid claim can be a right only if the former is combined with what it takes to satisfy the claim, i.e. with appropriate course of action.

According to Martin, the nature of moral right is that it has to be appropriately promoted and enforced if it is not to remain as nominal right. Correspondingly, its non-promotion or non-enforcement infirms it as a right. If the thing which qualifies the morally valid claim as a right (i.e. the morally approved ways of acting) is taken away, then it would fail to be a right at all. Thus human right as moral right requires the appropriate ways of acting, i.e. the *practices* of recognition and promotion. And this is *internal* to the concept itself. As an operative idea, the recognition and promotion of human rights are necessarily to be taken into consideration, for this determines whether any such right has been instantiated. Since a human right as a morally valid claim would remain as mere valid claim from moral perspective unless it is instantiated, it follows that a human right is something more than a morally valid claim. Martin further argues:

> A morally valid claim, when effectively recognized and maintained, is a claim *plus* something else (the "something else" being precisely what is lacking in the claim considered simply as a claim). A claim is not defective in the absence of these things, but a right is. A human right is defective, not as a claim but as a right, in the absence of appropriate practices of recognition and maintenance. The absolute

35 R. Martin, "Human Rights and Civil Rights", in *The Philosophy of Human Rights*, p. 77.

36 Ibid.

> difference between morally valid claims and human rights, then, is that rights do, and claims do not, include such practices within their concept.[37]

The point is that a morally valid claim by virtue of its simple qualities may secure a way of acting and may be widely practicable, yet it lacks the status of a right for not having appropriate form of social recognition. It is not enough to lay stress on the claim and on the qualities which makes it a morally valid claim; it requires social recognition and promotion in order to qualify as a human right. In other words, a human-right claim having social recognition is still a claim and valid one but it cannot be elevated to the status of a human-right so long as it is not recognized and protected by particular societies through particular courses of action. In this sense, rights are moral in character. Thus human right as a morally valid claim secures ways of acting primarily by normative measures, which is different from the practices of recognition in law and maintenance by governmental action. At this stage, people come to believe that right-claim makes it possible for them to protect their vital interests. They come gradually to realize that right-claim is a morally valid one. Thus human right-claim gains wide acceptance and recognition by the members of a particular society. As a result, people organize social movements to secure recognition and protection of rights against their own government, and thereby they make attempts to put an end to what they take to be the violation of human rights. So Martin argues for the practices of governmental recognition and promotion of human rights as part of the concept in question. He writes:

> On this view, the right is not just the claim, to which there are added the "called for" protective devices; instead, the right is the claim *as* recognized in law and maintained by

[37] R. Martin, "Human Rights and Civil Rights", in *The Philosophy of Human Rights*, p. 78.

> governmental action. And the issue whether something is a human right, or whether such rights "exist" or whether people "have" them, cannot be decided without consideration of the whole range of relevant practices, which include recognition in law and governmental maintenance of the claimed way of acting. Such practices are ingredient in the very notion of what it is for something to be a human right, or so my argument is meant to show.[38]

The point that human rights require the practices of recognition in law and maintenance by governmental action, Martin claims, has not been brought into the human rights picture whimsically or causally but as a result of an argument. The element of appropriate practices of recognition and maintenance is intrinsically contained in the very notion of human rights as the concept itself is an operative and action-demanding concept. Martin says:

> A human rights claim which lacks such recognition is still a claim, and may even be a morally valid one; but it cannot qualify as a human right.[39]

Thus we see that Martin conceives rights as following a developmental pattern in their evolution. Rights begin as requiring social protection of human good, and such protection is initially claimed by some person as moral entitlement. In the next stage, the right-claim is widely recognized and validated by the people of different societies, and the latter come to realize that right-claim really serves to protect their vital interests. And in the last stage, the right-claim gets recognition and maintenance of governmental institutions as right which *actually* serves peoples' interests.

Martin extensively argues in favour of the view that government is the principal addressee of human rights. We

---

38 R. Martin, "Human Rights and Civil Rights", in *The Philosophy of Human Rights*, p. 79.

39 Ibid.

would note here some of his arguments. In order to strengthen his arguments in this context, he argues against Cranston's view that human rights are rights of all individual *against all individuals*, with no mention of government at all. Martin accuses Cranston of ignoring history. He points out that the human rights manifestos are meant for imposing restraint upon governments. Though individuals are involved as beneficiaries of the restraints, the manifestos are not primarily addressed to them.

Martin also deplores Cranston's view that the right to fair trial as a human right is a right against all persons and not against government. Further, in case of what Martin calls "double-barrelled" human rights claims, such as the right to life, are addressed not only to all individuals but also to government in the form of legal security and enforcement for the protection of life. In this particular case individuals, along with state, are also the addressee of human rights. Moreover, Martin marks the human rights off from other moral rights by proposing government as the principal addressee of human right. He also disagrees with Bernard Mayo in this context. Though Mayo agrees that government is the principal addressee, but for him, this is so for "historical" reason rather than for "conceptual" reason. It is true that the conception of human rights has its origins at a certain age and undergone historical development but in course of historical development it has not borne the same meaning at different times. What Hobbes meant by "natural rights" may be different from what we today understand by the term "right". "But none of this justifies", Martin argues, "saying that governments and public law are subject to rights claims for reasons that are not contained in the notion of human rights."[40] For him, it is the conceptual reason (i.e. the very concept of human rights

[40] R. Martin, "Human Rights and Civil Rights", in *The Philosophy of Human Rights*, p. 81.

intrinsically possesses characteristics of recognition in law and maintenance by governmental action), that makes it the principal addressee of human rights.

In the conclusion of the article, Martin reiterates that the concept of human rights possesses an irreducible duality. On the one side, a human right is a valid claim, which is morally endorsable, practicable and supportable by relevant duties. It is a claim to some benefit and fully valid in its own right without entailing that it is recognized and maintained by those against whom the claim is made. On the other side, a morally valid claim is in need of recognition and maintenance by governmental *action* in order to be elevated to the status of a human right. The first dimension provides the moral foundation of rights while the second serves to maintain the integrity of the political–legal element, and the combination of both constitutes a full-fledged conception of human rights.

Conclusion

Among the five thinkers the views of whom we have dealt within the foregoing analysis, Green and MacDonald reject the conception of natural rights and develop their views on rights in their own unique ways. The remaining three thinkers – Wellman, Feinberg and Martin – have not criticized the natural-rights paradigm of rights but develop their views independently of it. For MacDonald, the utterances that concern ultimate social values like human rights are decisions as a result of human choices and preferences. If we think that human rights are beneficial for us, then they must be defended by means of arguments. And in order to defend the ultimate social values like human rights, we have to choose a side, i.e. to choose, for example, whether to defend liberty or slavery. This is more like choosing one's favourite poems, stories, work of art, etc. and not like choosing a scientific law, such as the uniformity of nature. But Wellman, following Hohfeldian model of legal rights, conceives analogous conception of ethical rights as a cluster of ethical liberties, claims, powers and immunities. Unlike Hohfeld who thinks that any of these elements is fundamental to a right, Wellman proposes that a right is constituted by these four normative elements together. What gives these elements a unity is the defining core or the essential element of a right. Human rights, according to Wellman, are a specific kind of ethical rights the addressee of which is the state.

Green and Feinberg recognize rights as possessing an irreducible duality. For Green, a right is both a claim of the individual and its recognition by the society. Similarly, for Feinberg, a right is a claim *to* something and *against* someone based on some legal or moral rules. For him, the claim has a primacy over duties. It is not a claim put forward merely as a claim but a *valid* claim. But Martin finds these conceptions as inadequate, for they do not include a course of action to be maintained by any agency like government. For him, in its evolution, a right begins with a claim of the individual as a moral entitlement, and then it gets a wide social recognition and finally, it requires promotion and maintenance by the governmental actions.

7

Human Rights and Utility

UTILITARIANISM is not the name of a single doctrine but a combination of several ethical theories. That is, it is a hedonistic, consequentialist, welfarist, maximalist and universalist doctrine. It is understood and used by different thinkers to establish their own theses which belong to different areas of human study, such as legal, political and ethical. Contemporary rights-discourse is one such area which has been immensely benefited by the arguments from utility. Though the classical utilitarian thinker, Bentham, was a staunch critic of the doctrine of natural rights and his posterior, Mill, talked little about the rights of man, but in recent times the different rights-thinkers have interpreted utilitarianism to suit their own purposes, and thus the rights-discourse has been greatly enriched by their contributions.

Among the thinkers who have made significant contributions to the rights-discourse by giving their own unique interpretations of utilitarianism are included D.G. Ritchie and David Lyons. Both Ritchie and Lyons formulate a synthesis between rights-theory and utilitarianism in their own respective ways. Though Ritchie rejects Bentham's highly individualistic approach to utility, he retains its conception of general welfare judged from social viewpoint. He modifies utilitarianism in terms of the process of natural selection and gives birth to a hybrid doctrine called "evolutionary utilitarianism". And rights, as valuable element of this doctrine, have been regarded as having social utility to bring about general welfare of people. But Lyons tries to find out an area of compatibility between rights and utility on the basis of his close reading of Mill. He makes an attempt to synthesize the utilitarian belief that moral norms are justified by their serving as effective means of advancing the general welfare of society and the belief in human rights. The objective of this chapter is to give a clear exposition of the rights-theories of both these thinkers.

Utilitarianism: An Overview

In order to facilitate the understanding of these two theories of rights it is worthwhile to begin with a brief analysis of utilitarianism in its pristine form which is based on the writings of Bentham and Mill. Broadly speaking, utilitarianism is a movement for legal, political and social reform which came into focus with the patronage and writings of Jeremy Bentham and John Stuart Mill in the first half of the nineteenth century. Following some of the eighteenth-century moralists like Butler and Shaftsbury who held that benevolence or seeking the good of others has a central place in moral life, the Scottish philosopher Francis Hutcheson actually said that the objective of good conduct is "the greatest happiness for the greatest number". Later, this phrase came to be the slogan of English utilitarians like Bentham and Mill. In its later developments, utilitarianism takes variety of forms, such as intuitional utilitarianism (Sidgwick) and ideal utilitarianism (Moore and Rashdall).

Let us first turn to the basic ideas of Bentham's utilitarianism which is regarded as "classical" version of the theory. Bentham is credited with the invention of the name "utilitarianism", but he did not originate the theory. He developed and formulated the fundamental principles of the doctrine. The sole objective of his life was to theorize and preach the ideal of utilitarianism, and thereby to bring about reforms in all departments of public life and to effect some increase of happiness in the lives of greatest number of people. Thus his theorizing of utilitarianism aims at having some utility in public life. Indeed, at the centre of his articulation of the theory lies the principle of utility that provides a standard by which our actions can be judged to be right or wrong. This theory judges all our actions according to their utility as means of promoting general happiness or prevention of general pain. Like Hobbes and other Enlightenment thinkers, he begins his theorizing with an account of human nature. For, he realizes that it is essential to understand the nature of men before drawing up a plan for reforms in social institutions that would serve the creatures like men. Bentham's most important ethical work, *An Introduction to the Principles of Morals and Legislation*, opens with a statement that expresses his view of human nature. He writes:

> Nature has placed mankind under the governance of two sovereign masters, *pain* and *pleasure*. It is for them alone to point out what we ought to do, as well as to determine what we shall do. On the one hand the standard of right and wrong, on the other the chain of causes and effects, are fastened to their throne. They govern us in all we do, in all we say, in all we think: every effort we can make to throw off our subjection, will serve but to demonstrate and confirm it. In words a man may pretend to abjure their empire: but in reality he will remain subject to it all the while.[1]

Bentham believes in fixed human nature. The pursuit of pleasure and avoidance of pain are what each human being wants in his life, and it is a fact of human nature that none can change or alter. The mode of pursuing pleasure and desiring the things of different kinds may vary from person to person but the fact remains that human beings cannot lead their lives without pursuing pleasure and avoiding pain. Pleasure and

---

1 J. Bentham, *An Introduction to the Principles of Morals and Legislation*, J.H. Burns and H.L.A. Hart (eds.), London: Methuen, 1982, p. 11.

pain, according to Bentham, are the "instruments" which are the motivating forces behind all human behaviour.

For Bentham, all actions should be judged as right or wrong solely according to their tendency to augment or diminish the utility, i.e. to promote happiness or prevention of pain. The principle of utility, which provides the standard of morality, recognizes the subjection of human beings to pleasures and pain, and thereby fulfils the utilitarian objective "to rear the fabric of felicity by the hands of reason and of law".[2] In his utilitarianism, Bentham advocates a hedonistic theory of value as, for him, pleasure is the only thing that is good in itself. All other things are valuable only if they contribute to the production of pleasure. Pleasure is understood by Bentham basically as a feeling or sensation which is the ultimate object of desire. "By utility", Bentham says:

> is meant that property in any object, whereby it tends to produce benefit, advantage, pleasure, good, or happiness, (all this in the present case comes to the same thing) or (what comes again to the same thing) to prevent the happening of mischief, pain, evil, or unhappiness to the party whose interest is considered.[3]

According to Bentham, the value of pleasure and pain can be measured in units. He develops a "felicific calculus" by means of which pleasure or happiness can be measured. This measurement of the value of pleasure and pain determines the utility of acts and enables us to compare them. For Bentham, there are seven "circumstances" by reference to which the value of pleasure or pain can be decided. These are: its intensity, duration, certainty or uncertainty, propinquity or remoteness, fecundity, purity and extent. These seven criteria

---

[2] J. Bentham, *An Introduction to the Principles of Morals and Legislation*, p. 11.

[3] Ibid., p. 12.

enable legislators or other agents to balance the sum of pleasures against the sum of pains and determine the best course of action. According to Bentham, this calculus should be kept in view as an ideal model of rational deliberation, so that the decisions conform as closely as possible and need not precede every moral judgement, every legislative or judicial operation. It follows from Bentham's theory of hedonism that he portrays man as naturally egoist, but at the same time he also advocates altruistic hedonism. For him, people become altruistic by the binding force of four sanctions – the physical, the political, the moral and the religious.

It is this Benthamite version of utilitarianism that is revised by John Stuart Mill – the major figure in the utilitarian tradition – in his *Utilitarianism*. His revisionism includes the partial defence and partial criticism aiming at the refinement of the "classical" doctrine. He begins by locating utilitarianism in the long history of moral philosophy and raising the age-old problems of the foundation of morality, determining the criterion of right and wrong and the supreme good of human life. He found it possible to find out the answers to these perennial questions of ethics in somewhat altered version of utilitarianism. Accordingly, he affirms that the principle of utility is capable of providing the proper foundation for morality and supply the criterion of right and wrong. And the happiness can also be accommodated as the *summum bonum* of human life within its framework. He writes:

> The creed which accepts as the foundation of morals, Utility, or the Greatest Happiness Principle, holds that actions are right in proportion as they tend to promote happiness, wrong as they tend to produce the reverse of happiness. By happiness is intended pleasure, and the absence of pain; by unhappiness, pain, and the privation of pleasure.[4]

---

[4] J.S. Mill, "Utilitarianism", in R.M. Hutchins (ed.) *Great Books of the Western World*, Chicago: Encyclopedia Britannica, 1952, p. 448.

This formulation has a close resemblance with Bentham's articulation of the basic principle of utilitarianism. In the same paragraph, Mill says that the standard version of utilitarianism is in need of further explanation. That is, it is not enough to accept the principle of utility as the supreme principle of morality and the happiness as the ultimate goal of human life; it is also particularly necessary to elaborate on the meaning of happiness as he understands it. For, it is the supplementary explanation particularly of "what things it includes in the ideas of pain and pleasure; and to what extent this is left an open question"[5] that would give a clear view of the moral standard it sets up. The philosophy of life on which this moral standard is grounded is the following:

> That pleasures, and freedom from pain, are the only things desirable as ends; and that all desirable things (which are as numerous in the utilitarian as in any other scheme) are desirable either for the pleasure inherent in themselves, or as means to the promotion of pleasure and the prevention of pain.[6]

While adhering to this philosophy of life, Mill intends to provide a somewhat altered version of utilitarianism which would respond to some objections generally raised against the doctrine. Mill and his predecessors are of the view that the good we seek to maximize consists in such mental states as pleasure or happiness. Yet Mill found it as his task to clarify the sense in which the term "pleasure" or "happiness" is to be used in his version of utilitarianism. He talks of "two very different ideas of happiness".[7] If the term "happiness" is taken to mean pure and simple feeling or state of pleasure, then it would make the doctrine vulnerable to the criticism that it is

[5] J.S. Mill, "Utilitarianism" in *Great Books of the Western World*, p. 448.

[6] Ibid.

[7] Ibid., p. 449.

"a doctrine worthy only of swine". It is in this sense that Bentham has actually employed the term. For Mill, this is inferior or lower pleasure. In contrast, Mill has taken the term "pleasure" to mean superior or higher pleasure. In this context, Wendy Donner writes:

> He (Mill) takes value to reside in complex mental experiences rather than sensations and he takes the quality of happiness as well as the quantity to be productive of its value. Mill's qualitative hedonism is a complex mental state account of utility which takes into account the quality as well as the quantity of pleasurable experiences in measuring their value and stands as a sophisticated alternative to Bentham's quantitative hedonism.[8]

In order to repudiate the charge that utilitarianism is a doctrine worthy of swine, Mill lays stress on the *quality* of pleasure, although without ignoring its quantitative dimension. The philosophy of life, which proposes that there is no higher and nobler end in human life than pleasure, was originally preached by the Epicureans whom Mill refers to. In keeping with the Epicurean view, Mill argues:

> . . . if the sources of pleasure were precisely the same to human beings and to swine, the rule of life which is good enough for the one would be good enough for the other. The comparison of the Epicurean life to that of beasts is felt as degrading, precisely because a beast's pleasures do not satisfy a human being's conceptions of happiness. Human beings have faculties more elevated than the animal appetites, and when once made conscious of them, do not regard anything as happiness which does not include their gratification.[9]

---

[8] W. Donner, "Mill's Utilitarianism", in John Skorupski (ed.) *The Cambridge Companion to Mill*, Cambridge: Cambridge University Press, 1998, p. 257.

[9] J.S. Mill, "Utilitarianism", in *Great Books of the Western World*, p. 448.

Mill says that the Epicureans also attach higher values to the pleasures of the intellect, feeling, imagination and moral sentiments than those of mere sensations. For him, the principle of utility is quite compatible with the fact "that some *kinds* of pleasure are more desirable and more valuable than others".[10] According to Mill, it is an "unquestionable fact" that those who enjoy both lower and higher pleasures prefer the kind of life that provides them the latter pleasures. Mill further argues that all human beings possess a sense of dignity to some extent roughly in proportion to their higher faculties, which obliges everyone to prefer higher pleasures. Mill attaches value to those people who are more inclined to enjoy higher pleasures than those who are happy and content with lower pleasures. "It is better to be a human being dissatisfied than a pig satisfied; better to be Socrates dissatisfied than a fool satisfied."[11] Human beings often indulge in inferior pleasures because of the infirmity of their character, but this does not show that they do not know what is preferable to them. For Mill, though both quality and quantity of pleasure matter but quality matters more. It is on the basis of these arguments that Mill finds Bentham's proposal that pleasure is to be measured only in terms of quantity and not in terms of quality as absurd and ridiculous.

Mill's objective of insisting on the qualitative dimension of pleasure is to argue for a better social and cultivated life of human persons as he believes that the self-developed persons are much more likely to promote good in the world as well as to lead satisfactory lives. For him, human persons through the pursuit of superior pleasure will be able to lead a refined and cultivated life, and also can play the role of educating general public as to how to cultivate and refine their tastes and talents, and thereby maximize happiness that life has to

---

[10] J.S. Mill, "Utilitarianism", *Great Books of the Western World*, p. 448.

[11] Ibid., p. 449.

offer. Mill believes that everyone has the potential to elevate himself and become more cultivated and refined moral being, and the opportunity for the development and growth must remain open to all, irrespective of their status – be it social, political, economic or any other. For, it is the best way to increase the total sum of happiness and well-being of all people. Mill discovers two factors that make life unsatisfactory, and these are: selfishness and the lack of mental cultivation. The excitement of life for those who care for nobody but themselves are much more diminished and curtailed in value. And also the lack of intellectual, artistic, or moral development make people unhappy and leave them dissatisfied in their lives. About the latter, Mill says:

> A cultivated mind – I do not mean that of a philosopher, but any mind to which the fountains of knowledge have been opened, and which has been taught, in any tolerable degree, to exercise its faculties – finds sources of inexhaustible interest in all that surrounds it; in the objects of nature, the achievement of art, the imagination of poetry, the incidents of history, the ways of mankind, past and present, and their prospects in the future.[12]

Taking "happiness" in its higher sense and giving it a special status, Mill wants all-round development of human individual, and this individual development, he believes, would result in cumulative development of a community and nation over time.

In this context, Mill also asks the question: What is the sanction of the principle of utility? Or what can motivate one to obey the dictate of the principle of utility? He ignores Bentham's list of four external sanctions – the physical, the political, the popular and the religious – as irrelevant to morality. He lays emphasis on what he calls "internal sanction". He describes it as

---

[12] J.S. Mill, "Utilitarianism", *Great Books of the Western World*, p. 451.

> a feeling in our own mind; a pain, more or less intense, attendant on violation of duty, which in properly cultivated moral natures rises, in the more serious cases, into shrinking from it as an impossibility.[13]

Mill calls it the subjective feeling in man's mind – the contentious feeling of man, which is the sanction of all morality.

Finally, Mill turns to the objection to utilitarianism that it is sometimes in conflict with the demands of justice, i.e. justice and utility are opposed to each other. Here, Mill gives an analysis of rights and defends this account in his theory. Though rights are not foundational in any form of utilitarianism but are grounded on human well-being, they have secured a strong defence in Mill's version. He makes a distinction between morality and expedience as follows:

> We do not call anything wrong, unless we mean to imply that a person ought to be punished in some way or other for doing it; if not by law, by the opinion of his fellow creatures; if not by opinion, by the reproaches of his own conscience. This seems the real turning point of the distinction between morality and simple expediency. It is a part of the notion of Duty in everyone of its forms, that a person may rightfully be compelled to fulfil it. Duty is a thing which may be *exacted* from a person, as one exacts a debt.[14]

Thus a morally wrong act justifies punishment for the wrong-doer while an inexpedient act does not. For example, to steal a cell phone from someone's pocket is morally wrong but to deprive someone of your charity is not but an inexpedient act. Hence punishment is the criterion of morality but not for those acts which are inexpedient. According to Mill, charity is an imperfect duty to which a right does not correspond. But

---

[13] J.S. Mill, "Utilitarianism", *Great Books of the Western World*, p. 458.

[14] Ibid., p. 468.

there are perfect duty in virtue of which a correlative *right* is attributed to some individual or individuals to whom the duty is owed. This latter feature constitutes the difference between obligation of justice and other moral obligations. In Mill's words:

> In the more precise language of philosophic jurists, duties of perfect obligation are those duties in virtue of which a correlative *right* resides in some person or persons; duties of imperfect obligation are those moral obligations which do not give birth to any right.[15]

Thus Mill defines moral right in terms of moral obligations. For him, an individual person has a moral right to something if there is a moral obligation on society to protect him in his possession of that thing. And Mill uses the idea of rights in analysing the concept of justice. For him, obligation of justice is distinguishable from moral obligations in general in that the former corresponds to the existence of rights. As Mill writes:

> Justice implies something which it is not only right to do, and wrong not to do, but which some individual person can claim from us as his moral right. . . . Wherever there is a right, the case is one of justice.[16]

To have a right, Mill says, is "to have something which society ought to defend me in the possession of". If someone asks, why should society defend me in this way? Then Mill replies: "I can give him no other reason than general utility".[17] To protect the rights of an individual person is one of the vital tasks of a society. For, rights give us security which is of paramount importance. But upholding rights of a person is

---

15 J.S. Mill, "Utilitarianism", *Great Books of the Western World*, p. 468.

16 Ibid., p. 469.

17 Ibid., p. 471.

not an absolute value. Mill acknowledges that there may be particular cases in which, a right and therefore justice, may be infringed. It may be, for example, a just act to steal food or medicine or to kidnap only one available doctor to save a life. But these acts directly violate someone's right to property or doctor's right to liberty. It is the appeal to the principle of utility that allows one to disrespect the rights to property and liberty in this case, according to which, we should act in ways that promote the greatest happiness of the greatest number. But, according to Mill, this is not to allow utility to prevail over justice. In cases like the above, justice demands that we do the thing in the way which is normally considered to be wrong.

Evolutionary Utilitarianism and Rights

Ritchie's book *Natural Rights* opens up with a historical review of various conceptions of natural law and natural rights that dominated the political and ethical theories from the Greeks down to the eighteenth century. In the fifth chapter, he turns to the criticism of the traditional conception of natural law and natural rights and presents his own view on rights. To begin with, Ritchie takes recourse to quotations from others' writings to define what a right is in both legal and moral senses. By legal rights, he understands a capacity of an individual to influence and control the actions of others with the approval and assistance of the state. The legal right is a kind of claim made by a person to restrain others' actions, and this is approved by the law of the land. The law of a state stands behind and entitles him to make such a claim upon other citizens. In the similar fashion, a moral right is meant to be a capacity of a person to impose restraint upon others' conduct with the concurrence and assistance of, at least having no opposition from, public opinion. The claim of a right in moral sense is in need of approval and backing from private individuals only, regardless of state's recognition. The point here is that there may well be disputes and disagreements with regard to both legal and moral rights. But while there are courts to make appeal to resolve the disputes and disagreements in case of legal rights, there is no such courts for moral rights where appeal can be made to have a abiding decision. It is due to the imprecise nature of moral rights that it becomes difficult to determine with regard to what cases and to what extent a person can enjoy moral rights. Besides, the prevalent public opinion change and differ with regard to moral matters, and this makes the situation further complicated.

According to Ritchie, it is in order to obviate these difficulties, the moral and political philosophers presume the law of nature and natural rights to be the ideal standard with reference to which all moral and political rights could be deduced. According to Ritchie:

> Natural rights are not identical with moral rights, because in many cases people have claimed that they had a natural right to do things that were not recognized either by the law of the land or by the prevalent public opinion or by the conscience of the *average* individual. Natural rights, when alleged by the would-be reformer, mean those rights which in his opinion would be recognized by the public opinion of such a society as he admires, and would either be supported or at least would not be interfered with by its laws, if it had any laws; they are the rights which he thinks ought to be recognized, i.e. they are the rights sanctioned by his ideal society, whatever that may be.[18]

The fundamental question he raises now is: "What determines rights?". He right away rejects the external authority of any form as the basis of natural or fundamental rights, and in this

---

18 D.G. Ritchie, *Natural Rights*, London: George Allen & Unwin, 1924, p. 80.

context he criticizes Hobbes. Appealing to nature too, according to Ritchie, cannot provide us with an ideal standard on which rights can be founded. Like Bentham, Ritchie rejects the law of nature as the court of appeal to settle the rights of man. He also refuses to ground the rights of man on the greatest happiness principle following Bentham. The difficulty that arises for him with regard to the law of nature is that of interpreting the "voice" of nature. For the law of nature admits of no analysis by rational means. To make an appeal to the law of nature means rejecting all attempts to argue from experience. Thus Ritchie rejects the law of nature and brings in the idea of "utility" to find a possible ground for the consideration of rights.

According to Ritchie, people are not agreed as to the meaning of the term "useful" as they are not with regard to what is right or just according to the law of nature. But the term is not something incapable of further analysis like the law of nature. Says Ritchie:

> It is true, the "useful", taken by itself, is quite as ambiguous as the just. But the useful does not profess to be something incapable of further analysis. It is confessedly a relative term, useful *for* something. Useful *for what?* It is here that the utilitarian theory stands in most in need of revision and correction.[19]

According to Ritchie, since the law of nature has failed to provide us that fundamental standard without which a society is impossible to remain integrated, we have nothing left except falling back upon human society itself as the last resort. That is, in order to maintain a minimum of security and harmony in human society, human rights are to be decided by appealing to social utility rather than by appealing to the law of nature. The well-known utilitarians in the history of philosophy are

[19] D.G. Ritchie, *Natural Rights*, p. 94.

Bentham and Mill who, in opposition to both authority and the law of nature, established "the greatest happiness of the greatest number" as the ethical standard with clear focus on individualism. Although Bentham rejects the conception of natural rights as "nonsense upon stilts", he retains abstract individualism in his theory according to which human beings are what he calls "moral atoms", and their nature is fixed and similar at all times and in all places. Ritchie rejects Bentham's greatest happiness principle along with his individualism as the ground for the rights of man and argues for a sort of Idealist ethical position. According to this position,

> . . . our particular self or *ego* is only the imperfect realization of a universal reason, one and indivisible throughout the universe, though manifested in countless forms and revealed most clearly to us, not in the movements of the stars, nor in the record of the rocks nor even in the upward striving life of plant and animal, but in the work of the human spirit, that is to say in the social institutions, in art, in religion, and where thought seeks to be at home with itself – in the meditations of the philosopher – if this be so, every human being may claim a right to be considered as such, because he *potentially* shares in this consciousness of the universal reason; he may claim the opportunity of developing this potentiality as far as possible.[20]

Clearly enough, such a theory does not believe in human nature as something fixed and immutable as the classical utilitarianism assumes it to be, but allows for a growth and development of human nature. A human being is capable of expanding his individual self through partaking in the one "Reason" or "Nature" and thereby realizes himself as an end-in-himself. And this realization becomes possible only through his participation in self-reflective process that finds expression

---

20 D.G. Ritchie, *Natural Rights*, pp. 96-97.

in art, religion, literature, etc. According to this theory, a society is assumed to have a *continuous* life of its own maintained by its individual members through partaking in its multifarious activities. Though an individual member is born and dies within it, but its own life continues. It is in course of time that the natural gifts and capacities of an individual or of a society as a whole are discovered. It is the end of the state, among other things, to provide the opportunity of developing the potentiality of individual members of a society.

Now, Ritchie points out that the conception of evolution, particularly the theory of natural selection, has a bearing upon our social life. This theory has corrected the errors as well as defended the utilitarian theories of morality and politics. According to the theory of social evolution, the good for any particular society lies in its continual struggle for existence with nature and other societies, and that which prevents such success of society is evil. The difference between social and natural evolution is that the former is no longer blind and mechanical process, but a self-reflective process that proceeds through critical reflections. Human beings through their participation in this self-reflective process gradually come to understand themselves and their situation better. It is again this self-reflective process that enables them to appreciate their role and the sphere of action as individual members in society, and their qualities and capacities as individuals.

Let us now proceed to understand the implications of this approach of Evolutionist Utilitarianism for the theory of rights. Classical Utilitarianism, on the one hand, conceives society as consisting merely of certain number of human individuals, each possessing a fixed and unchangeable nature. On the other, the advocates of natural rights theories think of society as an association of individuals joining together to secure respective natural rights which they are supposed to have been enjoyed in the state of nature. But both of them treat human beings as *discrete* individuals, lacking intrinsic social character. The rights and duties of each of these individuals are also decided from their individualistic standpoint. But Ritchie, being an Evolutionist Utilitarian, lays stress on human sociability and argues for the rights and duties to be decided from the perspective of society. Ritchie writes:

> The transition from Individualist to Evolutionist Utilitarianism – a transition which is being accepted by the great majority of writers on scientific ethics, from whatever point of view they set out – makes what one may call a "Copernican" change in our way of considering the question of rights. The eighteenth-century thinkers looked on society as made by individuals joining together, in order to secure their pre-existing natural rights. Unless we remain uninfluenced by the more scientific conceptions of human society now possible to us – we see that "natural rights", those rights which *ought to be* recognized, must be judged entirely from the point of view of society. We must return to the method of Plato: in order to know what is really just, we must call up a vision of an ideal society.[21]

Ritchie claims here to have brought about a "Copernican" change in the way the Classical Utilitarian conceives the idea of rights. People before Copernicus believed that the sun moved round the earth. But Copernicus introduced the opposite hypothesis that the earth itself moved round the sun. Similarly, Ritchie claims to have brought about a Copernican change by introducing the view that rights are to be decided from the point of view of society as whole against the classical utilitarian position that rights are to be recognized and judged from the standpoint of individual.

Ritchie understands human society in evolutionary terms, i.e. the society is always changing in terms of growth and

[21] D.G. Ritchie, *Natural Rights*, p. 101.

development, and this evolution of society differs from mere natural evolution in being no longer a blind and mechanical process but a self-conscious process. Individuals participating in this self-reflective process are no longer discrete individuals as they are regarded by individualist thinkers but having *social* nature. He is born into this world as a mere animal, and it is in society where he grows into a *rational* animal. It is in his participation in concrete social life that he becomes a moral person, i.e. he can have rights and duties only in relation to other members of the society. So whatever rights and duties he is allowed to have is to be decided only, according to Ritchie, from the societal standpoint and not vice versa. In his own words:

> "Nature", we might say, falling back on the antithesis, made man an animal; society has made him a rational animal – thinking, intelligent being, capable of moral action. The person with rights and duties is the product of a society, and the rights of the individual must therefore be judged from the point of view of a society as a whole, and not the society from the point of view of the individual.[22]

But the appeal to social utility that is proposed by Ritchie is not same as appealing to the law of nature, for the former is capable of further analysis but the latter is not. The social utility of entire human enterprise along with men's qualities and capacities can be analysed in the light of historical experience. To make an appeal to social utility means appealing to something that can be tested by experience. We learn from our past experience. It is from the latter that we anticipate our future course of action and decide our rights in varying social conditions. The advantage of the Evolutionary Utilitarianism is that it is always in favour of rational interpretation of experience on the basis of which human rights are to be decided

---

[22] D.G. Ritchie, *Natural Rights*, pp. 101-02.

instead of appealing to "dumb" Nature as the Classical Utilitarianism proposes. The reflections on social evolutionary process enable men to evaluate their situation and accordingly change their perspective. In the process of rational interpretation of experience, he discovers new rights which he is entitled to enjoy.

Revisionist Utilitarianism and Rights

A general objection raised against utilitarianism is that it cannot accommodate any conception of rights within its framework. For the general welfare standard, which is preached by utilitarianism, is essentially defective. And rights and general welfare principle cannot go hand in glove together. But, for Lyons, the ground on which the conclusion is reached is very weak, and it seems like a dogma rather than based on strong philosophical arguments. He takes it as his task in the article "Human Rights and the General Welfare" to challenge this dogma by attempting to repudiate the presumption that utilitarian belief that moral norms are justified when they are committed to serve the welfare of the society is in clash with the belief in rights and justice. In other words, he wants to explore the connection between human rights and general welfare. And he avowedly intends to accomplish this task by means of a close reading of the writings of the most famous utilitarian thinker, John Stuart Mill.

Lyons begins by pointing out that the concept of rights has not received much favour from the utilitarians. Bentham, the main patron of the utilitarianism, puts forward a bitter critique of rights (which we have discussed in Chapter IV). He believes in the command theory of rights, i.e the theory according to which rights can be rights only when they are enforced. As a legal positivist, he recognizes only legal rights, and hence there cannot be any unenforced rights like *moral* rights. Utilitarians even think that the infringement of rights is justified if that is necessary to bring about the smallest increase in the general welfare to the greatest number of people. For them, the infringement of rights does not necessarily depreciate the value of general welfare. It is due to these and other reasons that the utilitarians find the commitment to general welfare standard as opposed to the recognition of rights. But Lyons intends to show in this article as to how Mill challenges such a conclusion and accommodate both general welfare and rights in his theoretical framework. Though we have seen in the above discussion that in Chapter V of his *Utilitarianism* Mill very briefly stated his conception of rights, but Lyons's interpretation of Mill makes latter's view more clear and explicit as also brings out its various implications.

To begin with Lyons's interpretation of Mill, it may be relevant here to briefly state the distinction that is made between act-utilitarianism and rule-utilitarianism. On the one hand, an act-utilitarian holds that one is to judge what is right and what is wrong by appealing directly to the principle of utility, which says that an action is right that tends to produce the greatest balance of happiness over pain to the greatest number of people. On the other, according to rule-utilitarians, rules are central to morality. We are generally to tell what to do in a particular situation by invoking a rule or norm like that of truth-telling, the general compliance of which, in the long run, would maximize the general welfare of society. In case of rule-utilitarianism, we are supposed not to ask what particular action but what rule or norm that will tend to promote the general welfare of society. Thus the point is *not* that which action has the greatest utility but that which rule or norm has. However, in both act- and rule-utilitarianism, the principle of utility remains the ultimate standard of judging what action or rule will tend to produce the greatest happiness of the greatest number of people.

According to Lyons, Mill advocates a kind of rule-utilitarianism. For him, we ought to perform certain moral obligations, because the performance of these moral obligations would promote the general welfare of society. If we fail to carry out these moral obligations, then it would be reckoned as moral wrongs. And this would justifiably call for punishment. But, for Mill, there is another kind of acts which are called "inexpedient" acts as distinguished from wrong acts. Inexpedient acts are those which are unable to promote the general welfare. Thus to call an act wrong it is not enough to show that it is inexpedient, i.e. it fails to promote general welfare in the most efficient and productive manner possible, but one must have to argue that some sort of punishment would be justified for the person responsible for wrongful behaviour. These punishments would include both external sanctions, such as legal penalties and social disapproval as well as internal sanctions, such as guilt-feeling and pangs of conscience. Moral rules prohibiting wrongful behaviour, according to Mill, must be framed and make people comply with this rule the breach of which would justify some sort of punishment.

As Lyons interprets Mill, rights correspond only with the obligation of justice. When someone violates the rights of another person it would be an unjust act but act can be wrong without being unjust. It may be wrong *not* to be generous or charitable as these acts impose obligations on us. But these obligations do not correspond with rights. For, our being generous or charitable cannot be another's right. On Lyons view of Mill, "rights entail corresponding obligations".[23] Hence, Lyons argues that Mill's overt analysis of rights is to

[23] D. Lyons, "Human Rights and the General Welfare" in M.E. Winston (ed.) *The Philosophy of Human Rights*, Belmont: Wadsworth Publishing Company, 1989, p. 209.

be understood in terms of moral obligations. In order to clarify Mill's view, Lyons quotes from Mill the following:

> When we call anything a person's right, we mean that he has a valid claim upon society to protect him in the possession of it, either by the force of law or by that of education and opinion. If he has what we consider a sufficient claim, on whatever account, to have something guaranteed him by society, we say he has a right to it.[24]

In other words, when we say that someone has a moral right, this implies that another person or persons are under a beneficial obligation towards the right-holder. In response to the query as to why society would guarantee rights to a person? Mill invokes his utilitarian view that a society defends his rights only on the ground that these rights would promote the general welfare of that person, and this way of defending an individual's rights would serve some interest of that person. As Lyons says:

> Mill holds that someone has a right when he ought to be treated in a certain way, which serves (or refrains from undermining) some interest of his. Combining this with Mill's theory of obligation, we get the view that someone has a moral right when another person or persons are under a beneficial moral obligation towards him; or in other words, when there are sufficient grounds for the widespread internalization of a value that requires corresponding ways of acting towards him.[25]

Now, Lyons turns to the implications of Mill's commitment to rights and corresponding obligations. For him, since Mill admits that an individual's claim is validated by the general

---

[24] D. Lyons quotes this passage from Mill's "Utilitarianism". See his article "Human Rights and the General Welfare", in *The Philosophy of Human Rights*, p. 209.

[25] D. Lyons, "Human Rights and the General Welfare", in *The Philosophy of Human Rights*, p. 210.

welfare standard, i.e. the claim that would serve some interests of a person by protecting him, so he commits himself to a conception of rights. This conclusion is reached, Lyons points out, "from a reasonable interpretation of the general welfare standard coupled with a plausible analysis of rights".[26] Further, Lyons also claims that Mill's conception of rights is "superior" to that of Bentham as there are differences in their views on obligations. Though Bentham, like Mill, subscribes to the view that to have rights is to be benefited from another's obligation, he takes obligation in the sense of authorized coercion, which might not be justified. But Mill is at liberty to recognize rights in moral, rather than in legal, sense. Lyons argues not only to show that the utilitarian like Mill need not be averse to rights but also to stress that he is rather committed to an account of rights. The obligation that concerns justice and that corresponds with rights is formulated in terms of high-priority moral rules than those of merely useful obligations. For, Mill asserts that they "concern the essentials of human well-being more nearly, and are therefore of more absolute obligation, than any other rules for the guidance of life".[27] The rights that concern our most vital interests are the rights to freedom of action and security of person, which make possible a minimally acceptable condition of human life. The obligation of justice is more demanding than moral obligations in general in that it requires us to behave with other people in such a manner that would serve their vital interests, such as the freedom of action and security. As Lyons interprets him, Mill seems to agree that moral rules that serve to protect the demand of justice generally take priority over other moral rules. For, they are designed to serve the most vital interests of mankind. Though they are not "inviolable" this cannot easily be justified.

---

[26] D. Lyons, "Human Rights and the General Welfare", in *The Philosophy of Human Rights*, p. 210.

[27] Ibid., p. 211.

Conclusion

Having made a survey of utilitarianism, we have analysed the theories of rights as put forward by Ritchie and Lyons. According to Ritchie, social utility is the key conception on the basis of which human rights are to be judged. Here, the social utility is not to be taken in the sense that is given to it by Classical Utilitarians but has to be understood in terms of Evolutionary Utilitarian's sense of the term. In the latter's sense, the social utility does not mean merely having rights and institutions that are conducive to general happiness but means having those fundamental rights that are relevant to certain stage of social development to prevent the society from disintegration. Unlike Classical Utilitarians, Ritchie holds that these fundamental rights will vary in various stages of social development. As society is taken by Ritchie to be always moving forward and elevating itself to a next stage of development, the old set of rights loses its social utility and the need for new set of rights is felt. And rights are decided in varying stages of social development, according to Ritchie, on the basis of rational interpretation of experience. Besides, we have also seen that Lyons accommodates a conception of rights in his interpretation of Mill's utilitarianism. In his interpretation of Mill, Lyons not only rebuts the presumption that rights are opposed to considerations of social utility but also shows that utilitarians are committed to some conception of rights. He finds it reasonable to interpret Mill's analysis of rights in terms of moral obligations. As Lyons interprets Mill, there are certain moral obligations which we ought to perform the breach of which justifies punishment. These obligations concern justice, and they correspond with moral rights.

8

Human Rights, Moral Diversity and Indian Thought

It is an inescapable fact that the concept of human rights has its origin, foundation and development in the Western intellectual tradition, which we have analysed and considered so far. The Western thinkers and philosophers, beginning with the Greeks down to the present era, have contributed to the process of development and enrichment of the doctrine of human rights. Even the UN Declaration of Human Rights, 1948, together with later Covenants, has been drafted keeping mainly in view the Western conception of human rights. The Westernness of human rights conception and its so-called universality have remained an important issue throughout the process which has led to the framing of UN Declaration of Human Rights. While affirming the Westernness of human rights some recent thinkers have cast doubt about the claim of its universality. This doctrine may be called universal if it aspires to ascribe a *single* set of rights to all men irrespective of their national origin, gender, culture, religion and the like. But it cannot claim itself to be a universalist doctrine if it intends to assert the universal rights in a world that is characterized by "diversity of morals". For, the latter is inconvenient, if not anti-thetical, to the universality claimed for human rights. In order to make the idea of human rights a universally *accepted* norm it is necessary to loosen the idea from the shackles of Western modernism and to reconstruct it with due emphasis on non-Western perspectives as well. While arguing in line with this view, we would discuss the Kantian conception of human dignity and also present a case study from the Indian tradition which provides an articulation of human dignity on the basis of a particular Vedāntic dictum *tat tvam asi* (That thou art). That is, we would see that the concept of human dignity has two *different* conceptions: one is articulated by the Western tradition, and the other is developed by the Eastern tradition.

Human Rights and Moral Diversity

The problem that arises in claiming universality for an operative idea like human rights is that despite its origin in a particular socio-cultural milieu it aspires to be applied to the entire globe irrespective of different moral virtues, principles and practices which people have obligation to follow in their respective societies. In such a situation, to claim the universality for human rights is to claim its universality in *abstraction*, i.e. without taking into consideration the different moralities of the global societies. So in order to make the idea of human rights globally an accepted norm there is need to claim its universality based on the faiths and values of the major civilizations of the world. The concept of human rights should remain open to the enrichment and articulation based on various perspectives given by different traditions and world-views. As Denial A. Bell observes:

> I certainly wouldn't want to deny the possibility that East Asians, or anyone else, can make a substantial contribution to an international order based on universally accepted human rights. After all, human rights have been in constant evolution, and we should welcome the possibility of further positive contributions to this process.[1]

---

1 D.A. Bell, *East Meets West*, Princeton: Princeton University Press, 2000, p. 105.

Every moral idea is closely associated with history, politics and culture of a particular tradition, and the notion of human rights is not an exception. At the different stages of historical, political and cultural development, a tradition may wake up to diverse forms and variety of human rights. Now, if certain standards of human rights that arise out of a particular tradition are defined in terms of its inherent values and beliefs, and then the people of all other traditions are demanded to comply with them, then this would be grossly unfair. If the contemporary understanding of human rights based mainly on Western values and beliefs are taken as expressing final and unchanging truths and demanded from other traditions of the world to comply with them, then this would imply the devaluation of other religious and cultural traditions. For,

> The aggressive promotion of a universal standard of human rights is sometimes viewed as a paternalistic attempt to impose alien Western values. In any event, human rights must be developed within understandings of specific people's culture, community and traditions. The concept of human rights should not, however, be frozen in time, but rather be a dynamic principle, capable of adapting within a complex, varied and changing global society.[2]

As human rights are defined keeping mainly in focus the Western values and beliefs, such as the Western imperialist history, individualism and rationalism, it would not be proper to apply this model to other cultural and religious traditions which are dominated by different sorts of values and beliefs. For example, unlike the Western nations, India has suffered a colonial agony, and having values and beliefs that are based on its spiritualism. Now, if such a tradition is demanded to be rigidly complied with the Western conception of human

---

[2] South Asia Human Rights Documentation Centre, *Introducing Human Rights*, New Delhi: Oxford University Press, 2006, p. 5.

rights, then it would be unjustified. For, this would imply the utter disregard for its age-old cultural and religious tradition.

Since the history, culture and political contexts are different in various regions of the world, there is need to have human rights with *regional* resonance. While some of the human rights that have universal character may be shared by the people of all traditions of the globe (e.g. the right to life, the right to environment), but some new ideas of rights have to be conceived on the basis of the values, beliefs and political contexts of the tradition in which it is to be practised (e.g. the rights relating to family, which is not everywhere the same). Thus the universal character of human rights has to be combined with *regional* resonance in order to meet the requirement of a particular tradition and the different issues that are given priority at a particular point of historical period.

Though the idea of human rights with a philosophical perspective has its origin in Western intellectual tradition, this notion is found to be embedded in all major cultural traditions of the world in diverse forms. The ideas that people should be treated in accordance with certain standards, and the ideas of human dignity and worth are not confined to the Western modernist culture alone, though this very term "human right" may not always be employed.[3] The other intellectual and religious traditions of the world too are fertile enough to be able to contribute towards reconstruction of human rights conception. Upendra Baxi points out:

> Every societal culture contains beliefs, sentiments, symbols that impart sense to the notion of being human, no matter in how many different registers of inclusivity. Every societal culture, similarly, has traditions of understanding concerning what rights a human being ought to have. No

---

[3] J. Ife, *Human Rights and Social Work*, Cambridge: Cambridge University Press, 2001, p. 2.

> culture, then, is devoid of notions about human rights, even when what constitutes these rights varies within the same culture in time and place and they vary across comparable cultures.[4]

So far we have suggested that given the diversity of morals it is necessary to provide the notion of human rights a dynamic, inclusive and cross-cultural character, and in this effort one cannot deny the fact of moral diversity in the world.[5] Let us now clarify the idea of moral diversity that permeates the global societies.

Morality is coeval with social life, and if we identify human rights as a moral idea, then we must make sense of the moral inheritance of various societies of the world to discover the way people are treated with dignity and honour. In such an effort we inescapably encounter the fact that morality is not the same in every society. Members of a certain society are obliged to follow a set of virtues, rules and practices, which differ from those of the other societies. For example, the morality that is followed in urban England is different from what is practised in rural India. In certain respects, morality of today's India differs markedly from what it was used to be in the medieval India. Thus the world in which we live is characterized by moral diversity. The latter inheres in different religious, political, social and other forms of life. This is basically the diversity of faith and value that matters most in upholding a uniform mode of life in the world, and it is this diversity that is troublesome for accommodating human rights in different modes of peoples' lives.

---

4 U. Baxi, *The Future of Human Rights*, New Delhi: Oxford University Press, 2nd edn., 2006, p. 21.

5 Attempts to provide human rights dynamic, inclusive and cross-cultural character have already been made in recent years by such authors as Stephen C. Angle (*Human Rights and Chinese Thought*, Cambridge, 2002) and Arvind Sharma (*Hinduism and Human Rights*, Oxford, 2003).

Despite the diversity of morals it is not difficult to discover a common ground between various ideologies and practices, and the idea of human rights. For, the domains of ideologies and human rights are not mutually exclusive but rather overlap each other. There may be some religious or political truths, which may coincide with what the doctrine of human rights intends to preach. It is the issues of coincidence that are needed to be focused upon in order to strengthen the demands of human rights and thereby making the claim of human rights appealing to the world permeated by moral diversity. So let the people of various traditions of the world to interpret and understand the conceptions of human rights in their *own* terms and not necessarily in the terms dictated by the Western modernism. The interpretation of the moral inheritance of several cultural traditions would make for a global conception of human rights as a whole. In this age of globalization, the concept of human rights or ideas akin to it should be given a global and cross-cultural dimension to make this operative notion a more effective weapon for realizing the goal of humanity.

Closely linked to this idea of human rights is the notion of human dignity, which is derived from the Latin word *dignitus* – a word denoting the possession of higher social or political status, or the moral attributes associated with that status. Human rights are invoked in order to exemplify the dignity in the life of men. Thus possessing human rights enables a human person to lead a *dignified* and *respectful* life in society. Being human denotes living with a special moral status that distinguishes us from other animal species. In whatever conditions the humans may be, they are endowed with self-consciousness and hence are worthy of treated as subjects. This results in humans having dignity or worth intrinsically possessed by them. Human dignity – and the special value societies attach to the person – form the core, and ground the ascription, of what is called today human rights. The importance and recognition given to the idea of dignity in contemporary discourse of human rights are evident from several statements in the UN Declaration of Human Rights, 1948:

> Whereas recognition of the inherent *dignity* and of the equal and inalienable rights of all members of the human family is the foundation of freedom, justice and peace in the world.[6]

This recognition of the idea of human dignity as an underlying principle of contemporary conception of human rights has prompted many thinkers to explore it through various philosophical and religious traditions of the world. By stating that Adam was created in the "image of God", the Old Testament of the Bible bestows on humans a priceless dignity. The concept of dignity occupies a central place in Immanual Kant's moral philosophy as well – he confers a special value to humans by declaring that individuals are "ends in themselves". For Kant, humans have to be treated in a way that reflects their special value above anything else. For, it is an intrinsic and unconditioned quality of an individual. The bestowal of dignity on all members of the human race is found prevalent not only in the West, but it is also illustrated in other cultural traditions of the world. The Indian tradition too joins this chorus based on its ancient spirituality – the latter being its central motive and governing principle of its people. Generally speaking, Indian tradition gives an exalted place to human species in the universe of animate beings, plants and inanimate things. The Upaniṣads provide an elevated place to man by equating the soul of humans with the *Brahman* – the Supreme Reality. Modern Indian thinkers and reformers who belong to the Vedāntic tradition like Swami Vivekananda and Sri

---

6 "Preamble" of the Universal Declaration of Human Rights, 1948 in *Human Rights: A Source Book*, comp. and ed. Arjun Dev, Indira Arjun Dev and Sutapa Das, New Delhi: National Council of Educational Research and Training, 1996, p. 27 (my emphasis).

Aurobindo raised human dignity to a new height by providing a re-interpretation of the Vedāntic truth. What is distinctive of these thinkers is that they provide practical effect of the Vedāntic truth to the concrete life of illiterate, oppressed, underprivileged, downtrodden and poor masses of India and the world at large. In the present chapter a modest attempt will be made to analyse, from the present-day perspective, Vivekananda's interpretation of a particular Vedāntic dictum and its application to human life. This analysis presents Vivekananda as an apostle of what we today call "human rights".

The Kantian Conception of Human Dignity

Before I venture to analyse the Vedāntic conception of human dignity it is worthwhile to present Kant's philosophical articulation of the idea of human dignity, which is considered to be the comprehensive and fullest account available in the Western tradition. Human dignity was a central ethical value in the Enlightenment era of the early modern Europe. The expression generally means the fundamental worth of every individual person. It is a quality of person that entitles him to be regarded and respected by others. Kant has retained this general meaning but develops it further in his own way in his ethics.

Let us begin by analysing basic points of the Kantian ethics, which are relevant to the understanding of his conception of human dignity. Kant's theory of ethics is avowedly called the "metaphysics of morals". A "metaphysics" is, for Kant, a body of pure and a priori knowledge which prescribes a priori principles of morality relating to human action. According to Kant, we are capable of willing to do something, and this willing takes place either under the influence of our kernel impulses or inclinations, or by virtue of our rational motive. Whenever we will to do something under the influence of impulses or inclinations, then such actions cannot be rated as *moral* actions. On the contrary, whenever an action is motivated by our rational nature, then such an action attains the status of a moral action. A moral action, for Kant, must have an "objective ground" for its willing, and this objective ground is what is called by Kant "end". According to Kant, some ends are merely "subjective" and they depend on impulses or inclinations. But some ends are "objective" and they depend on our rational motive that is valid for all human beings. It is needless to mention that a motive refers to some kind of thought which moves us to will something, and the objective end is that towards which a motive is directed.

The will is that which initiates an action. It is not mere wish to do something; it means taking a decision to act or perform according to a maxim – the latter being the subjective principle of action. But the ground of its determination does not lie in itself. Nor does it have its locus in the nature of man or in the circumstances of the world in which the agent is placed, but in what Kant calls "the pure practical reason". It is Reason in its practical use or function which determines the will. The practical reason exerts its influence on the will by means of the moral imperative. The influence under which an imperative is issued by the will is what Kant is meant by rational motive. This rational motive concerns something that is not valid because something else is valued but something that has "absolute worth". The thing that has absolute worth is, for Kant, an "end in itself". The latter is the unconditioned and objective ground of the moral law or what Kant calls "the Categorical Imperative". The rational nature of man, for having its absolute worth, is the end in itself. As Kant says: "rational nature exists as an end in itself".[7] He continues:

---

[7] I. Kant, *The Moral Law: Groundwork of the Metaphysic of Morals*, tr. H.J. Paton with a preface, commentary and analysis, London: Routledge Classics Edition, Indian repr., 2007, p. 106.

> This is the way in which a man necessarily conceives his own existence: it is therefore so far a *subjective* principle of human actions. But it is also the way in which every other rational being conceives his existence on the same rational ground which is valid also for me; hence it is at the same time an *objective* principle, from which, as a supreme practical ground, it must be possible to derive all laws for the will.[8]

What this passage amounts to is the following three-step argument: Since (a) every rational being necessarily regards himself as an end in itself, and accepts that (b) every one else is justified in regarding himself as an end in itself, (c) it is therefore an objective principle that everyone should be treated as an end in itself. The move from (a) to (b) is made possible by universalizing the rational nature as existing in everyone else. The point to be noted here is that the rational nature or Reason is not taken to be specific to particular individuals but exists in everyone else as *impersonal* reason. Hence in (c) we find an objectively valid ground to treat every human being as end in itself, which follows from (a) and (b).

Accordingly, Kant formulates the following imperative which is known as "the humanity principle":

> Act in such a way that you always treat humanity, whether in your own person or in the person of any other, never simply as a means, but always at the same time as an end.[9]

Here, the use of the adverb "simply" is important. Kant's point is *not* that we should never use human persons as means at all. Our day-to-day life would be impossible unless we make use of one another. Every time I read a book I make use of the author, every time I write I make use of people who have

---

[8] I. Kant, *The Moral Law*, p. 106.

[9] Ibid., pp. 106-07.

produced pen and paper, and every time I drink tea I make use of who prepares a cup of tea for me. Thus examples could be multiplied. What Kant stresses here is that we should not regard human persons *simply* as means to our own ends. All human persons – honest or dishonest, educated or illiterate – are ends in themselves, and we should treat them as such. A thing is that which is used merely as means, but persons are such that they are always needed to be considered as ends in themselves. A person who contemplates suicide due to painful circumstances, Kant says, should ask himself as to whether his action is consistent with the humanity principle. In his attempt to commit suicide he is using himself as a means and not as an end in itself.

Kant has put forward the following justification for treating person as end in itself. For him, nature is a system of natural ends which are hierarchical in character. That is, one natural end is dependent on another end, in the sense that one end exists for the sake of another. For example, insects exist as food for fish and fish exists as food for man, and thus the hierarchical order of ends ends with man, for "man is the final end of creation".[10] In other words, neither man as rational being exists for the sake of anything else nor he possesses value in relation to anything else. Rather, he possesses supreme value as an end in itself, and all other ends exist and possess value for the sake of man. This status of man as prevailing over all other ends is what entitles him to possess "dignity".

Now, what precisely is the nature of human dignity in Kant's ethics? Kant's theory of morals is basically concerned with providing human beings with a status above anything else. In what Kant calls "the kingdom of ends", persons are to

---

[10] I. Kant, *Critique of Judgement*, tr. with Analytical Indexes by J.C. Meredith, Oxford: Clarendon Press, 1986, p. 99.

be respected as ends in themselves, and hence as possessing dignity. He contrasts "value" and "dignity". Kant writes:

> In the kingdom of ends everything has either a *price* or a *dignity*. If it has a price, something else can be put in its place as an *equivalent*; if it is exalted above all price and so admits of no equivalent, then it has a dignity.[11]

His point is that whatever has a price or a value can be rationally sacrificed or exchanged for something else which has an equal price or value. "Price" is possessed by all the various individual objects of desire, such as material goods or personalities such as skill, or diligence, or humour, or strength. If I buy a parker pen and immediately lost it, and if someone then presents me a parker pen which is exactly the same as the previous one, it will be just as good as my earlier parker pen and I will have lost nothing. The same is true of personal qualities. If I have intellectual skills and this may be, to some extent, compensate me for my lack of skill as a singer. It is because of the role that such things play in our lives, they possess value. But it is the person who gives value to these things. Hence a thing and a person should have different kinds of worth for each of them:

> What is relative to universal human inclinations and needs has a *market price*; what, even without presupposing a need, accords with a certain taste – that is, with satisfaction in the mere purposeless play of our mental powers – has a *fancy price* (*Affektionspreis*); but that which constitutes the sole condition under which anything can be an end in itself has not merely a relative value – that is, a price – but has an intrinsic value – that is, *dignity*.[12]

Like the value of a thing or a personal quality, the dignity of

---

[11] I. Kant, *The Moral Law: Groundwork of the Metaphysic of Morals*, p. 113.

[12] Ibid.

man does not have market value or fancy value, and therefore it cannot be exchanged, replaced, or compensated for anything else. Further, in case of a thing or a skill a person can promote its value by means of campaigning or advertising the product or may develop the skill through rigorous training. But the human dignity cannot be promoted or developed as it is *already* possessed by the persons since their birth, whether he is honest or dishonest, intelligent or foolish. Thus thing has market value or fancy value, but dignity is the highest ethical value possessed by persons, which demands sheer respect from other persons with no material gain. In the Kantian ethics, respect for moral law or the Categorical Imperative as the law of reason is identical with the respect that we feel for rational beings as ends in themselves.

The Vedāntic Conception of Human Dignity

Now, we shall turn to the explication of the Vedāntic dictum "That thou art" (*tat tvam asi*) in order to show as to how it provides a ground for understanding human dignity. Unlike the European modernist culture that has set the standard of life based on materialism and consumerism, the differentiating character of Indian culture has its spirituality as the core and foundation. And the perennial issues of Indian life are shaped by the spirit and mould of spirituality. Again, the European culture is in search of truth in the physical sciences by means of reason, but the ancient Indian culture's quest for truth is not confined to the world of space and time but goes beyond it to achieve spiritual Self-knowledge. It is this plane of spirituality that provides the broad framework for the treatment of all inanimate things and animate beings in certain standards. While identifying the spirituality as governing principle of Indian civilization, Sri Aurobindo writes:

> The whole root of difference between Indian and European culture springs from the spiritual aim of Indian civilization.

> It is the turn which this aim imposes on all the rich and luxuriant variety of its forms and rhythms that gives to it its unique character. For even what it has in common with other cultures gets from that turn a stamp of striking originality and solitary greatness. A spiritual aspiration was the governing force of this culture, its core of thought, its ruling passion.[13]

In keeping with this spiritual tradition, the human individual has been given an elevated place in Indian thought by proclaiming him as part of the Divine or *Brahman*. In *Chāndogya Upaniṣad,* we find the dictum *tat tvam asi* (That thou art) which means that the *ātman* (self) in all beings is identical with the supreme Self.[14] In this Upaniṣad, there is the story of Śvetaketu, a boy who after completing his education in his *guru*'s house returned home. To test his knowledge, his father Uddālaka asked him some fundamental questions that the boy could not reply. Then, Uddālaka began to teach his son thus: "In the beginning all this was Existence (*Sat*), one only, without a second". "That (Existence) saw, I shall become many". Then that Existence (*sat*) manifests Itself into the manifold universe; therefore the origin of everything in Creation is Divine, is that Existence. As this statement would have remained merely a hypothesis unless it was ascertained by some evidence, Uddālaka gave his son various concrete examples of it, each time concluding his statements by saying that *Brahman* is identical with Śvetaketu's self: *Tat tvam asi, Śvetaketu.* Uddālaka's purpose of identifying the Supreme Reality with the self of his son is very positive, and that is to make Śvetaketu realize that one's self is self-evident and needs no

---

13 Sri Aurobindo, *The Foundations of Indian Culture*, Pondicherry: Sri Aurobindo Ashram, 8th impression, 1995, p. 121.

14 Swami Lokeswarananda (ed.), *Chandagya Upanishad*, chapter VI, section XVI, Calcutta: The Ramakrishna Institute of Culture, 1998, p. 579.

proof from outside. That is, the statement that the *sat* is the source of the whole universe is required to be invested with certitude, and that is provided by Śvetaketu's own introspection that his individual self is a part of the Universal Self. However, this does not, in any way, give rise to any confusion to Śvetaketu that his individual self is the source of the manifold world, but rather the Universal Self that is represented by his spatio-temporal existence. By affirming the identification of individual self and *Brahman*, the status of a person is ennobled. This conception has clearly been brought out by I.C. Sharma as follows:

> According to the Upaniṣads man is regarded as the *highest* reality, because of all the creatures of the world it is he who is self-conscious and most anxious to become infinite. In spite of finitude and imperfection man feels a great urge to attain infinity and perfection. This keen desire to go from the limited to the unlimited, from the mortal to the immortal, and from the relative to the absolute state of existence is indicative of the fact that man's real self is not the individual self but the universal self. The innermost nature of man is not contradictory, relative and pluralistic existence, but it is non-contradictory, absolute and non-dualistic reality. In other worlds, man is potentially God, and the aim of all ethics is to convert this potentiality into an activity, manhood into Divinity, and relativity into Absoluteness. This is what is meant by self-realization as the goal of the Upaniṣadic ethics.[15]

Humans, whose reality is the *ātman* (self), are endowed with the divine light and power of the *Brahman*. This Reality is without distinction – such as religious, linguistic, racial, sexual, national or social. Though Indian society has always stressed

[15] I.C. Sharma, *Ethical Philosophies of India*, ed. and revised by Stanley M. Daugert, Ghaziabad: International Publishing, Duhai, Indian repr., 1991, p. 94 (my emphasis).

on the status of the individual in a social hierarchy, the identification of the individual with the Divine provides a *dignity* that places any person above all social customs and strata. The human race has been addressed by the Upaniṣads as *amṛtasya putrāḥ* (the children of immortality). This recognition of unique significance and dignity of each individual and his sacredness in Indian thought is an important contribution towards understanding of human rights conception. This Vedāntic conception of human dignity has been emphasized by Sri Aurobindo, Swami Vivekananda and other contemporary thinkers of India in clear and elegant terms. Sri Aurobindo writes:

> The *dignity* given to human existence by the Vedāntic thought and by the thought of the classical ages of Indian culture exceeded anything conceived by the Western idea of humanity. Man in the West has always been only an ephemeral creature of Nature or a soul manufactured at birth by an arbitrary breath of the whimsical Creator and set under impossible conditions to get salvation, but far likely to be thrown away into the burning refuse-heap of Hell as a hopeless failure. At best he is exalted by a reasoning mind and will and an effort to be better than God or Nature made him. Far more ennobling, inspiring, filled with the motive-force of a great idea is the conception placed before us by Indian culture. Man in the Indian idea is a spirit veiled in the works of energy, moving to self-discovery, capable of Godhead. He is a soul that is growing through Nature to conscious selfhood; he is a divinity and an eternal existence; he is an ever-flowing wave of the God-ocean, an inextinguishable spark of the supreme Fire.[16]

Vivekananda concurs with this Vedāntic truth, yet he differs on laying emphasis on various aspects of the dictum. He thought that emphasizing the divine origin of human beings would serve

[16] Sri Aurobindo, *The Foundations of Indian Culture*, p. 98 (my emphasis).

to make Vedānta practical and would enable the Indian masses to regain their lost faith. For him, human beings comprise both physical and spiritual dimension. His physical dimension consists of a biological and psychological system and much more developed than other beings, as it exhibits a better organic unity and purpose; this, however, is considered humans' lower nature. The spiritual dimension relates to the *ātman* of an individual which is beyond the psycho-physical organism. This is person's higher nature. In this context, Vivekananda writes:

> And Man, the Infinite, Impersonal Man, is manifesting Himself as person. We the infinite have limited ourselves, as it were, into small parts. The Vedānta says that Infinity is our true nature; it will never vanish, it will abide for ever.[17]

According to Vivekananda, *Brahman* is Impersonal, is one. This one Reality is reflected in men as manifold. In order to clarify this point, he takes the Vedāntic analogy of *pratibimba* (reflection). Here the *Brahman* is compared with the sun which may shine in its reflections on water kept in different vessels, but all these reflections of the sun in water are apparent – the real sun is beyond these reflections in water. Likewise, the light of *Brahman* is reflected in every man, and thereby he is elevated to the status of Highest Reality. Vivekananda says:

> The only God to worship is the human soul in the human body. Of course all animals are temples too, but man is the highest, the Taj Mahal of temples. If I cannot worship in that, no other temple will be of any advantage. The moment I have realized God sitting in the temple of every human body, the moment I stand in *reverence* before every human being and see God in him – that moment I am free from bondage, everything that binds vanishes, and I am free.[18]

---

17 *The Complete Works of Swami Vivekananda*, Calcutta: Advaita Ashrama, Mayavati Memorial Edition, 1992, vol. II, p. 323.

18 *The Complete Works of Swami Vivekananda*, vol. II, p. 321 (emphasis mine).

But, like Vedānta, he does not regard the embodied existence of man as entirely false. For him, the embodied state of man is the foundation and is in need of development and perfection in order to achieve the spiritual goal. Vivekananda considers the human physical dimension as follows:

> This human body is the greatest body in the universe, and a human being the greatest being. Man is higher than all animals, than all angels; none is greater than man.[19]

Vivekananda does not see the restatement of the Vedāntic identification of man with the *Brahman* as his only task but to give it a practical direction in men's lives, and hence his is practical Vedānta. He combines the Vedāntic truth with practice. He was not a philosopher in the traditional sense of the term to remain satisfied with mere intellectual exercise but a faithful messenger of ancient Indian truth and culture with a mission. And this mission was to uplift the condition of mankind in all spheres, such as social, economic and religious. He felt that the human person as the embodiment of Godhead was in dire need of uplift in terms of social, economic and religious dimensions. He drew on the Vedāntic idea to emancipate the masses from poverty, weakness and social evils, which he came to realize after an extensive travel undertaken by him throughout India. It is his first-hand experience of *de*humanizing social, economic and religious conditions of the Indian masses that led him to reinterpret Vedānta. Thus at the centre of his falling back upon the Vedāntic truth is the restoration of self-confidence in man who is primordially a reflection of the divine entity. In other words, Vivekandanda's emphasis on the Vedāntic identification of man as the true abode of divinity was to exalt the *dignity* of man in the world. He realized that it would be of no use to have the knowledge of Vedāntic truth unless and until it was

[19] *The Complete Works of Swami Vivekananda*, vol. I, p. 142.

not reflected in compassionate behaviour towards the low-caste, downtrodden or poor people. He decided to put the Vedāntic truth at work for the millions of poor and downtrodden people suffering from hunger, ignorance, disease, prejudice, etc. Vivekananda realized the stark reality of Indian masses as he wrote:

> The nation is sinking, the curse of unnumbered millions is on our heads – those to whom we have been giving ditch-water to drink when they have been dying of thirst and while the perennial river of water was flowing past, the unnumbered millions whom we have allowed to starve in sight of plenty, the unnumbered millions to whom we have talked of Advaita and whom we have hated with all our strength, the unnumbered millions for whom we have invented the doctrine of Lokācāra (usage), to whom we have talked theoretically that we are all the same and all are one with the same Lord, without even an ounce of practice.[20]

It pained him to see that while we preached the Vedāntic egalitarianism, there existed the vast disparities between rich and poor, high caste and low caste, literate and illiterate, privileged and downtrodden. His woeful awareness of human degradation in various forms gave rise to his interest in the re-interpretation of Vedānta and thereby providing the philosophical foundation of his actions that were directed towards reducing the distressing differences among the people. Guided by the Vedāntic truth, he dedicates his life to the service of God in *human* form to emancipate them from injustice, fear and evil, and thereby enable them to regain the faith in themselves. His expression "Daridra-Nārāyaṇa" (God the poor) to refer to the deprived and poor masses indicates that he equated the service of the poor with the service of God in terms of its importance and value. He exhorts people to seek God in men and worship them as reflections of the *Brahman*.

---

20 *The Complete Works of Swami Vivekananda,* vol. III, p. 431.

Again, his famous phrase "*Jīva* is Śiva" indicates that he held the human person in high esteem, but for him, this was not enough. The human persons, he heartily felt, are in dire need of benevolent services in terms of personal, social, economic and spiritual needs, and accordingly he responded to the changing secular and spiritual needs of the society, which are intensely felt with the passage of time. He was not a so-called spiritual *guru* whose only task is to preach the spiritual truth to the common people, but a *karma-yogin* of highest order, who initiated the actions towards the uplift of mankind. He included in the range of his services to the masses the economic, social, spiritual benefits. Grounded as he was in the lofty truths of Vedānta, he made a down-to-earth approach to the perennial problems of the masses. He declared:

> What we want is not so much spirituality as a little of the bringing down of the Advaita into the material world. First bread and then religion. We stuff them too much with religion, when the poor fellows have been starving. No dogmas will satisfy the cravings of hunger.[21]

Thus Vivekananda took a holistic approach to the perpetual problems of mankind and tried to find the best solution for them.

In view of the foregoing analysis, Vivekananda can very well be regarded as an apostle of what we today call 'human rights'. If we regard the dignity of man as the core and foundation of human rights, then Vivekananda obviously lays the stress on dignity and sacredness of man as being the abode of divinity based on the Vedāntic spiritualism. He did not remain satisfied to see the Vedāntic egalitarianism as being merely preached throughout the ages in India but felt the urgent need to sharpen its focus by giving it a new interpretation in order to apply it to the concrete social life of

[21] *The Complete Works of Swami Vivekananda*, vol. III, p. 432.

man. He provides a broad theoretical framework based on Vedāntic egalitarianism for the treatment of human beings in highest possible standard in their earthly lives. It is on this account of the Vedāntic analysis of human dignity that he can be called to be a human-rights thinker.[22]

Conclusion

What is argued in brief in the present chapter is that human rights in this age of globalization are needed to be understood discursively. That is, the understanding of this concept will be based on different cultural traditions of the world. It is not necessarily to be understood in the terms dictated by the Western modernist culture. For, we believe that different cultural traditions of the world have their own conceptions of rights and dignity and are potential grounds for articulating their own conceptions, although these very terms may not always be used by them. What is needed now is to investigate the moral inheritance of the different cultural traditions of the world and thereby bring out their significance for humanity. This process of investigation into the depths of moral traditions would gradually contribute towards a more

---

22 It seems that in today's parlance, Vivekananda can also be regarded as a human rights *activist* as well for his sincere crusade against all forms of oppression, prejudice, ignorance, penury, etc. In keeping with his Vedāntic understanding of human dignity, he dedicates his life to the service of what he calls "God in human form". His practical Vedānta reconciles spiritualism with the material life and thereby aims at fulfilling both the secular and spiritual needs of the society. He initiates determinate actions to restore men's inner spiritual dignity without which he would sink into the cesspool of sin and disorder that are the condition of earthly existence. He felt the urgent need to render the compassionate service to the oppressed, ignorant and poor people and thereby to bring about changes for good in the life of men in their different dimensions. It is with this solemn objective in mind that Vivekananda set up the Ramakrishna Mission in 1897 and gave a concrete and institutional shape to his social service programme.

inclusive and cross-cultural conception of human rights, and thereby it would help realize the goal of humanity.

While briefly arguing in line with this view, we have presented two conceptions of human dignity – one is from the Kantian tradition and the other is from the Vedāntic tradition. In these two traditions, the *same* concept, i.e. the concept of dignity holds two *different* conceptions, which is regarded as an important underlying principle of human rights. On the one hand, Kant pleads for treating human beings as ends in themselves and not as means to anything else. It is the treatment of human beings as ends in themselves, which constitutes the dignity of human beings as distinguished from the market value or fancy value of material things. On the other, the Vedānta equates human beings with the *Brahman* or the Supreme Reality and thereby the status of them is ennobled. The Vedāntic thinkers, such as Sri Aurobindo and Swami Vivekananda highlighted this Vedāntic truth by providing a re-interpretation of the Vedānta.

Bibliography

Angle, S.C. (2002): *Human Rights and Chinese Thought: A Cross-cultural Inquiry*, Cambridge: Cambridge University Press.

Baxi, U. (1987): *The Right to be Human*, Delhi: Lancer International in association with India International Centre.

——— (1994): *Inhuman Wrongs and Human Rights* Delhi: Har Anand.

——— (2006): *The Future of Human Rights*, 2nd edn., New Delhi: Oxford University Press.

Beitz, C. (2003): "What Human Rights Mean", *Daedalus*, Journal of the American Academy of Arts and Sciences, Winter.

Bell, D.A. (2000): *East Meets West*, Princeton: Princeton University Press.

Bentham, J. (1982): *An Introduction to the Principles of Morals and Legislation*, ed. J.H. Burns and H.L.A. Hart, New York: Methuen.

Brandt, R.B. (1983): "The Concept of a Moral Right and Its Function", *The Journal of Philosophy*, vol. LXXX, no 1.

Brenkert, G.G. (1986): "Marx and Human Rights", *Journal of the History of Philosophy*, vol. XXIV, no. 1.

Brown, S.M. Jr. (1955): "Inalienable rights", *The Philosophical Review*, vol. LXIV, no. 2.

Buchanan, A.E. (1982): *Marx and Justice: The Radical Critique of Liberalism*, London: Methuen.

Burke, E. (1910): *Reflections on the Revolution in France*, London: Everyman's Library.

Campbell, T. (1983): *The Left and Rights*, London: Routledge and Kegan Paul.

Cranston, M. (1973): *What Are Human Rights*, London: The Bodley Head.

Davidson, S. (1993): *Human Rights*, Buckingham: Open University Press.

Donnelly, J. (1985): *The Concept of Human Rights*, London: Croom Helm.

——— (1989): *Universal Human Rights in Theory and Practice*, London: Cornall University Press.

Eterovich, F.H. (1972): *Approaches to Natural Law: From Plato to Kant*, New

York: Exposition Press.

Falk, R. (2000): *Human Rights Horizons: The Pursuit of Justice in a Globalizing World*, New York: Routledge.

Feinberg, J. (1989): "The Nature and Value of Rights" in Morton Winston (ed.) *The Philosophy of Human Rights*, Belmont: Wadsworth Publishing Company.

Fennessy, R.R. (1963): *Burke, Paine and the Rights of Man: A Difference of Political Opinion*, The Hague: Martinus Nijhoff.

Ferry, L. (1990): *Rights: The New Quarrel Between the Ancients and the Moderns*, tr. Franklin Philip, Chicago: The University of Chicago Press.

Frankena, W.K. (1955): "Natural and Inalienable Rights", *The Philosophical Review*, vol. LXIV, no. 2.

Freeden, M. (1990): "Human Rights and Welfare: A Communitarian View", *Ethics*, vol. 100.

——— (1997): *Rights*, Indian repr., Delhi: World View Publications.

Freeman, M. (1994): "The Philosophical Foundations of Human Rights", *Human Rights Quarterly*, vol. 16.

Green, T.H. (1941): *Lectures on the Principles of Political Obligation*, London: Orient Longman.

Habibi, D.A. (2001): *John Stuart Mill and the Ethic of Human Growth*, Dordrecht: Kluwer Academic Publishers.

Harrison, R. (1983): *Bentham*, The Arguments of the Philosophers Series, London: Routledge.

Hart, H.L.A. (1984): "Are There any Natural Rights?" in Jeremy Waldron (ed.) *Theories of Rights*, Oxford: Oxford University Press.

——— (1982): *Essays on Bentham*, Oxford: Clarendon Press.

Herbert, G.B. (1977): "Human Rights and Historicist Ontology", *Philosophical Forum*, vol. IX, no. 1.

Hobbes, T. (1996): *Leviathan*, ed. with an Introduction and Notes by J.C.A. Gaskin, Oxford World's Classics, Oxford: Oxford University Press.

Ife, J. (2001): *Human Rights and Social Work*, Cambridge: Cambridge University Press.

Ishay, M.R. (ed.), (1997): *The Human Rights Reader*, London: Routledge.

Jones, P. (1989): "Re-examining Rights", *British Journal of Political Science*, vol. 19.

——— (1994): *Rights*, London: The Macmillan Press.

Jones, T. (2002): *Modern Political Thinkers and Ideas: A Historical Introduction*, London: Routledge.

Kamenka, E. and A.E.S. Tay (eds.), (1978): *Human Rights*, London: Edward Arnold.

Kolakowski, L. (1983): "Marxism and Human Rights", *Daedalus*, Journal of the American Academy of Arts and Sciences, vol. 112, no. 4.

Lee, W.L. (2002): *On Marx*, Belmont: Wadsworth Publishing Company.

Locke, J. (1993): *Two Treatises of Government*, ed. Mark Goldie, London: Everyman Edition.

——— (2008): *An Essay Concerning Human Understanding*, Oxford: Oxford University Press, Oxford World's Classics.

Lyons, D. (1989): "Human Rights and the General Welfare", in Morton Winston (ed.) *The Philosophy of Human Rights*, Belmont: Wadsworth Publishing Company.

——— (1994): *Rights, Welfare, and Mill's Moral Theory*, New York: Oxford University Press.

Machan, T.R. (1989) *Individuals and Their Rights*, Illinois: Open Court Publishing Company.

——— (1980): "Some Recent Work in Human Rights Theory", *American Philosophical Quarterly*, vol. 17, no. 2.

McCloskey, H.J. (1976): "Rights: Some Conceptual Issues", *Australasian Journal of Philosophy*, vol. 54, no. 2.

MacDonald, M. (1984): "Natural Rights", in Jeremy Waldron (ed.) *Theories of Rights*, Oxford: Oxford University Press.

Macfarlane, L.J. (1985): *The Theory and Practice of Human Rights*, London: Maurice Temple Smith.

Macpherson, C.B. (1962): *The Political Theory of Possessive Individualism: Hobbes to Locke*, Oxford: Oxford University Press.

Maritain, J. (1945): *The Rights of Man and Natural Rights*, London: The Centenary Press.

Martin, R. (1989): "Human Rights and Civil Rights", in Morton Winston (ed.) *The Philosophy of Human Rights*, Belmont: Wadsworth Publishing Company.

Martin, R. and J.W. Nickel, (1980): "Recent Work on the Concept of Rights", *American Philosophical Quarterly*, vol. 17, no. 3.

Marx, K. (1977): *Economic and Philosophic Manuscripts of 1844*, 5th edn., Moscow: Progress Publishers.

Melden, A.I. (1972): "The Play of Rights", *The Monist*, vol. 56.

Mill, J.S. (1952): "Utilitarianism", in R.M. Hutchins (ed.) *Great Books of the Western World*, Chicago: Encyclopedia Britannica.

Milne, A.J.M. (1968): *Freedom and Rights: A Philosophical Synthesis*, London: George Allen & Unwin.

——— (1986): *Human Rights and Human Diversity*, London: The Macmillan Press.

Miri, M. (2003): "A Note on the Idea of Human Rights", in *Identity and the Moral Life*, New Delhi: Oxford University Press.

Muschamp, D. (ed.), (1986): *Political Thinkers*, London: Macmillan Education.

Nelson, W.N. (1974): "Special Rights, General Rights, and Social Justice", *Philosophy and Public Affairs*, vol. 3, no. 4.

Ness, P.V. (ed.), (1999): *Debating Human Rights*, London: Routledge.

Nussbaum, M.C. (2001): "Public Philosophy and International Feminism" in C.P. Ragland and Sarah Heidt (eds.) *What Is Philosophy?*, New Haven: Yale University Press.

Paine, T. (1966): *The Rights of Man*, London: Everyman's Library.

Parekh, B. (1987): "The Modern Conception of Right and its Marxist Critique" in Upendra Baxi (ed.) *The Right to be Human*, Delhi: Lancer International.

Passos, J.D. (ed.) (2002): *The Living Thoughts of Tom Paine,* New Delhi: Rupa & Co..

Perry, T.D. (1985): "Two Domains of Rights", *Philosophy and Phenomenological Research*, vol. XLV, no. 4.

Philp, M. (1989): *Paine*, Oxford: Oxford University Press.

Popper, K. (1999): *The Open Society and Its Enemies*, vol. II, repr., London: Routledge & Kegan Paul.

——— (ed.), (1994): *In Search of Better World*, London: Routledge.

Ramsay, M. (1997): *What's Wrong with Liberalism?: A Radical Critique of Liberal Political Philosophy*, London: Leicester University Press.

Raphael, D.D. (1967): *Political Theory and the Rights of Man*, London: Macmillan.

Richards, B.A. (1968): "Inalienable Rights: Recent Criticism and Old Doctrine", *Philosophy and Phenomenological Research*, vol. XXIX.

Ricoeur, P. (ed.), (1986): *Philosophical Foundations of Human Rights*, Paris: Unesco.

Ritchie, D.G. (1952): *Natural Rights*, London: George Allen & Unwin.

Scarre, G. (1996): *Utilitarianism*, London: Routledge.

Schoeman, F. (1993): "Bentham's Theory of Rights", in *Jeremy Bentham: Critical Assessments*, vol. III, London: Routledge.

Shapiro, I. (1986): *The Evolution of Rights in Liberal Theory*, Cambridge: Cambridge University Press.

Sharma, I.C. (1991): *Ethical Philosophies of India*, ed. Stanley M. Daugert,

Indian repr., Ghaziabad: International Publishing, Duhai.

Skorupski, J. (ed.), (1998): *The Cambridge Companion to Mill*, Cambridge: Cambridge University Press.

——— (2007): *Why Read Mill Today*, London: Routledge.

South Asian Human Rights Documentation Centre (2006): *Introducing Human Rights*, New Delhi: Oxford University Press.

Sri Aurobindo (1995): *The Foundations of Indian Culture*, 8th edn., Pondicherry: Sri Aurobindo Ashram.

——— (1998): *The Human Cycle*, 3rd edn., Pondicherry: Sri Aurobindo Ashram.

Strauss, L. (1953): *Natural Rights and History*, Chicago: Chicago University Press.

Symonides, J. (ed.), (2002): *Human Rights: Concepts and Standards*, Indian repr., Jaipur: Rawat Publications.

Tuck, R. (1979): *Natural Rights Theories: Their Origin and Development*, Cambridge: Cambridge University Press.

——— (1989): *Hobbes: A Very Short Introduction*, Oxford: Oxford University Press.

Vivekananda, Swami (1992): *The Complete Works of Swami Vivekananda*, Mayavati Memorial Edition, 8 vols., Calcutta: Advaita Ashrama.

Waldron, J. (ed.), (1987): *"Nonsense Upon Stilts": Bentham, Burke and Marx on the Rights of Man*, London: Methuen.

——— (ed.), (1984): *Theories of Rights*, Oxford: Oxford University Press.

Wellman, C. (1989): "A New Conception of Human Rights", in Morton Winston (ed.) *The Philosophy of Human Rights*, Belmont: Wadsworth Publishing Company.

Winston, M.E. (ed.), (1989): *The Philosophy of Human Rights*, Belmont: Wadsworth Publishing Company.

——— (2007): "Human Rights as Moral Rebellion and Social Construction", *Journal of Human Rights*, vol. 6.

Index